OLYMPIA

THE SCULPTURES
OF THE TEMPLE OF ZEUS

PHAIDON

Frontispiece: Apollo.
See plates 105–9.

OLYMPIA

THE SCULPTURES
OF THE TEMPLE OF ZEUS

BY BERNARD ASHMOLE

Emeritus Professor of Classical Archaeology & Art in the University of Oxford

AND NICHOLAS YALOURIS

Ephor of Antiquities, Western Peloponnesus

WITH NEW PHOTOGRAPHS BY

ALISON FRANTZ

PHAIDON PRESS

MADE IN GREAT BRITAIN

TEXT PRINTED BY R. & R. CLARK LTD · EDINBURGH

PLATES PRINTED BY LONSDALE AND BARTHOLOMEW (LEICESTER) LTD · LEICESTER

BOUND BY A. W. BAIN & CO LTD · LONDON

CONTENTS

PREFACE

WHILE teaching the history of Greek sculpture in London, and afterwards in Oxford, for nearly thirty years, I had constantly felt the need for a simple, fully-illustrated account in English of the sculptures of the temple of Zeus at Olympia, which would serve as an introduction for students and for the many others who are interested in them.

Two or three years ago Miss Alison Frantz and I agreed that we would make a joint attempt to meet this need. There was, however, the difficulty that, since the original excavations, a great number of fragments had been added to the sculptures, many in recent years, and that whilst some of these had been published, others had not.

A happy solution was found when Dr. Nicholas Yalouris, Ephor of Antiquities for the Western Peloponnesus, who has charge of the museum at Olympia and has himself made many of the new additions, agreed to join us, and to take this opportunity of publishing them as the second part of the book. His section includes a sketch of the history of the piecing-together of the pediments and metopes, describes the new additions in detail and the inferences that can be drawn from them, and makes some general remarks on the composition and character of the sculptures which have occurred to him during the years that he has been at work. His views differ in several respects from mine, but we have made no attempt to bring them into line with one another, believing that it does no harm for a reader to realize that there is still room for discussion: it may cause him to look again and again at the sculptures and so deepen his knowledge and appreciation of them.

We wish to record our gratitude to many who have helped us in various ways: Dr. Yalouris to his wife for her assistance in translating, correcting, and checking his manuscript; to Mrs. R. Euelpides for some important information; to the artists St. Triantis and K. Perakis; also to the technicians A. Mavraganis, K. Pavlatos, Chr. Yannakopoulos, and the late J. Bakoulis, for the important contributions they have made in recognizing and attaching unidentified fragments from the store-rooms of the museum at Olympia; also to the artist A. Papaeliopoulos (for the drawings of the metopes); Miss Frantz and I to the Greek Archaeological Service, to M. Pierre Devambez of the Musée du Louvre for his courtesy and helpfulness; to Professor Homer Thompson; to Dr. I. Grafe; to Nicholas Restakis, who processed the photographs; to Ilias Andreou and the staff of the museum at Olympia; and, for photographs, to Dr. A. Greifenhagen, Dr. R. Noll, Dr. H. B. Schulz, Dr. D. von Bothmer, and Mr. Brian Cook. Finally, I should like to thank Professor Eduard Fraenkel for valuable criticism, and my wife for her constant and patient help.

BERNARD ASHMOLE

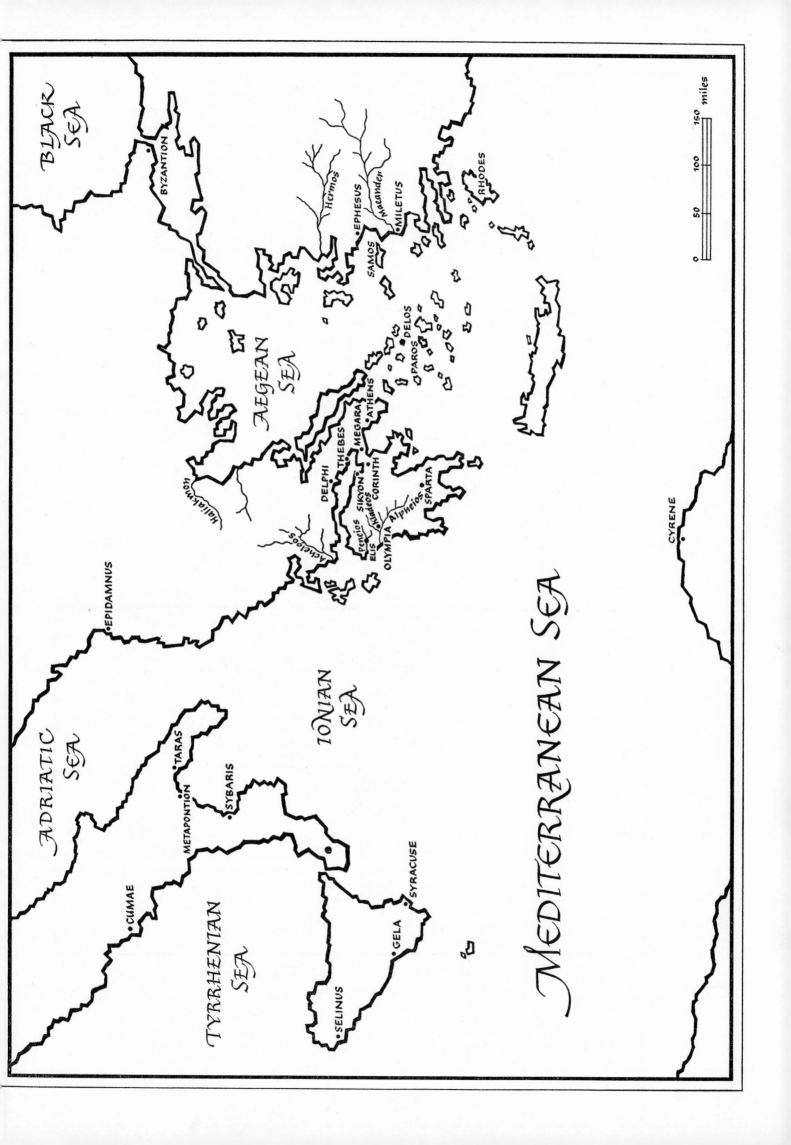

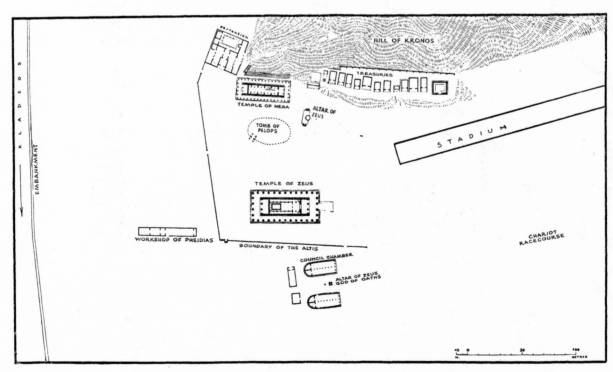

PLAN OF THE ALTIS AT OLYMPIA, 450 B.C.

OLYMPIA

THE SCULPTURES OF THE TEMPLE OF ZEUS

THE SITE

OLYMPIA lies in the north-western Peloponnese, about a dozen miles from the sea, in an open valley flanked by low hills, through which runs the river Alpheios. At this point it is joined by its tributary, the Kladeos, and to the east of the angle between them, at the foot of a small conical hill known as the hill of Kronos, is the sacred precinct, the Altis (fig. 1). Less than a mile away up the valley to the east is another hill, once the site of Pisa, a city which had for many years contested with Elis the control of the Olympic Festival. The Eleans destroyed Pisa about 470 B.C., but the name persisted as a poetic synonym for Olympia long afterwards.

Olympia, which was not a city but a sanctuary, had a fair claim to be regarded as the centre of the Greek world. Its patron deity was Zeus, the king of the gods, and less than a generation after the temple was built there arose within it an unsurpassed work of religious art, the colossal gold-and-ivory Zeus by Pheidias. Delphi may have had a deeper religious significance, but all in all, for religion, for athletics, and as a pan-Hellenic meeting-place, Olympia was supreme, and its geographical position made it readily accessible, not only to the cities of Greece itself, but to the Greek cities with which the coasts of Italy and Sicily were thronged.

At the end of the Persian wars, in the decade after 480, the Greeks had a desire for unity never felt so deeply before, and rarely since; and Olympia, not directly involved in the conflict but, unlike Delphi, above every suspicion of disloyalty, offered a natural focus for this sentiment.

The Festival had long been established as an event of capital importance in Greek life, but the appearance of the sanctuary must have seemed not quite worthy of this great and growing prestige. Its main features at that time were a primitive shrine called the tomb of Pelops and the Great Altar of Zeus, which was a hillock about twenty feet high composed entirely of ashes from the thighs of victims sacrificed to him over countless years. The only temple was the so-called Heraion, probably not a temple of Hera only, but of Zeus with Hera as his consort. This temple, situated almost at the north-western corner of the Altis, had been built in wood in the seventh century B.C., and had been reconstructed in the sixth, in stone, sun-dried brick and timber, with a wooden colonnade round it which was now undergoing a piecemeal reconstruction in stone. Clearly the sanctuary needed some dominating feature to mark its importance. (See plan on p. 4, and fig. 6.)

Some such thoughts as these must have passed through the minds of the rulers of Elis, for when the destruction of Pisa brought them great wealth, they decided to use it for an entirely new temple, dedicated to Zeus alone. This was erected not quite centrally in the Altis but towards the south-west, on an artificial mound designed to raise it four or five feet above the surrounding level: and here it stood for close on a thousand years. During that time it suffered periodical damage from earthquakes: there were major repairs to both the structure and the sculptures about a century after it was built, and in the second or first century B.C.: and many minor ones throughout antiquity. Like most of the buildings on the site it was finally overwhelmed by flood-waters from the Kladeos and the Alpheios.

The first excavations were made by the French in 1829: they discovered and removed to Paris parts of several of the metopes. The excavation of 1876–82 by the German Archaeological Institute, which, except for scattered fragments discovered since, brought to light all the sculptures from the temple now in the museum at Olympia, was not so much concerned with the stratification of the pottery as a modern one would be, but otherwise it was a model, both in execution and in speed and excellence of publication. The four great volumes edited by E. Curtius and F. Adler, in the third of which Georg Treu published the sculptures of the temple, will never be superseded.

PAUSANIAS. Apart from the actual remains, our chief information about the temple comes from Pausanias, a Greek born in Lydia, who, in the mid-second century A.D. wrote a comprehensive guide-book for travellers to Greece. He was at Olympia in A.D. 174 and must have spent many days there, for there was much to record. He had the help of at least one local guide, and also had access to the records kept by the priests, so that we might expect his account to be especially accurate. As will be seen, we can detect one or two mistakes, and suspect others, but this is hardly surprising in view of the great number of monuments, and the vast amount of information about them which he had to digest. He tells us the date of the temple, and its architect, describes the two pediments, giving the name of the designer of each, and mentions the subjects of the metopes. All this is first-hand information, and of great value, since we have so little from other sources. The relevant passage from Pausanias is given on page 31 below.

THE TEMPLE OF ZEUS

DATE. With the help of Pausanias and the evidence of the excavations, we can fix the date of the building and its sculptures with a fair degree of accuracy. The Eleans defeated the Pisatans about 470 B.C. Some thirteen years later, in 457, at the battle of Tanagra, the Lacedaemonian alliance defeated the Argives, Athenians, and Ionians. To commemorate it the Spartans dedicated a golden shield on the topmost gable of the temple. A fragment of the inscription on marble that went with it has survived, and Pausanias recorded it fully. Now it is reasonable to assume that this dedication was made not long after the victory of Tanagra, and that the temple was completed by then: otherwise it would not have been possible or wise to fasten an extremely valuable object on the very top of it. That gives us a period for the whole project from about 470 to about 456. If we allow a year or two after the conquest of 470 for turning the booty from Pisa into ready money, devising the scheme, commissioning the architect, choosing the sculptors, assembling the craftsmen, and procuring the marble, it seems that the sculptures must have been carved in the dozen years between 468 and 456. The quarrying of stone for the temple and the building of it must have gone on at the same time as the carving: the metopes had to be inserted before the roof was on, but the pedimental figures need not have been placed in position until the last few months.

ARCHITECTURE. The architect was a local man, Libon of Elis, and the temple was pure Doric, both in design and in feeling – austere, logical, and majestic. Like all Greek temples it was designed primarily as the house of the god, not a place of congregation. It consisted of a single chamber to hold the cult-image, with a deep portico in front of the main entrance-door formed by the projecting side-walls of this chamber, and a similar portico at the back, but this gave no access to the temple; later, doors were fitted, and it may have served as a treasury. This nucleus was surrounded by a single colonnade of thirty-four Doric columns, six on each façade and – counting the corner columns twice – thirteen on each side. The temple stood on a platform of three steps, rather too high for ordinary use, and at the east end a ramp of masonry led up over them to the centre of the façade (figs. 2-6). The length overall was about two hundred feet. The material, except the marble tiles of the roof, was a local shelly limestone, coated with a fine white stucco composed chiefly of marble-dust: details of the column-capitals and of the entablature were coloured red and blue.

SCULPTURAL DECORATION. The sculptural decoration was simply and logically disposed. Outside, at each end, between the low-pitched roof and the top of the entablature, was a space which the Greeks called *aetos* – an eagle – and we a pediment. This was just over eighty feet long, rather over ten feet high in the centre, but narrowing down to nothing at the corners, and only three feet deep (fig. 4). Both these spaces were filled with sculpture. A large pediment presents two main problems: the first is to prevent the weight of the statues bringing down the floor: the second is to produce a unified design which will fill this rapidly narrowing field without gross discrepancy of scale between the central figures and those further out. Figures fully in the round, when over life-size, are apt to project too far for safety, so that even when these difficulties of comparative scale have been overcome it is not simply a matter of placing a series of statues inside a given frame: though apparently in the round, many of them are really in high relief, and their design has been adjusted accordingly.

Also on the outside of the temple, and running the whole way round it, was the normal Doric frieze consisting of metopes and triglyphs. On the Parthenon at Athens these metopes are sculptured in high relief, and there is something of a conflict both of scale and of interest between the figures in the pediments and those on the metopes. At Olympia this conflict was avoided by leaving the metopes blank: all interest was focussed on the pediments. But behind the outer row of columns, over the portico at each end of the building, there was another Doric frieze of six metopes, and these, nearly square and over five feet high, were sculptured in very high relief; the front series broke upon the view as the visitor walked up the ramp and stood between the two central columns of the façade; and there was a corresponding viewpoint for the six over the porch at the back (figs. 3–5).

COLOUR. All the sculptures were painted, probably in a few bold colours, with much use of red and blue: the flesh of the women must have been light in tone, but that of the men brown. The iris and pupils of the eyes were painted in. Some details, especially the surface of the hair, were left by the sculptor to be represented entirely in paint: there was no fixed rule about this, but it is more frequent in the metopes, possibly because the light was more diffused there and finely-carved detail would have been lost. The general effect must have been startlingly life-like, but sublimated by the colour-scheme and by the formal quality of the sculptures.

THE SCULPTURES OF THE TEMPLE

AUTHORSHIP. It is an index of how little we know about Greek sculpture, owing to its wholesale destruction in later times, that we should be unable to name, not only the sculptors but even the school of sculpture which produced this, one of the two or three most important series of Greek marbles now in existence. And it is tantalizing that Pausanias should have been so explicit in giving the names of the sculptors and so unhelpful about them otherwise. Pausanias says that the east pediment was by Paionios of Mende. Now we possess a work by Paionios, also at Olympia, a statue of Victory set up by the Messenians and Naupactians after the battle of Sphakteria, which was fought in 425. This statue was made, it is true, thirty or forty years after the temple, but even if we allow for that, there seems little in common between it and the sculptures of the east pediment. It is therefore usually assumed that Pausanias, whilst being taken round the site by his guide, misunderstood him when they were looking up at the east pediment and thought that he was referring to the pedimental sculptures when in fact he was referring to the central acroterion, the statue on the peak of the gable above him. This we know was by Paionios, for in the inscription on the base of the Victory of the Messenians he states explicitly that he won the competition for the acroteria of the temple.

Of the west pediment Pausanias says that it was by Alkamenes, and here again there is a difficulty, chiefly because our knowledge of the style of Alkamenes from other sources is scanty, and because what evidence we do possess shows that it had little in common with the style of Olympia. Some official at Olympia, whether it was Pausanias' guide or another, must have given him the name of Alkamenes, so that it looks as though that were the tradition there;

but this was six hundred years after the sculptures were carved, and we cannot be certain that the tradition had been continuous.

Whoever the sculptors were, the style is remarkably homogeneous. Most archaeologists will agree that it is not Athenian and not eastern Greek: the choice would therefore seem to lie between a local Peloponnesian school (though the lack of marble in the Peloponnese makes it unlikely that there was a large school of marble-sculptors there), a northern Greek school, or one from the Cyclades, where there were, as we know, skilled marble-workers and productive quarries, from one or more of which, on Paros, the marble for the sculptures of the temple came. Some ancient authors say that Alkamenes was an islander, so the truth may lie there; but it is a very tenuous clue.

METHODS OF CARVING. Closely connected with this problem is another, that of how exactly the sculptures were made. Here again we have virtually no written evidence, and are forced to draw inferences from the basic physical conditions, which are these. Parian marble is exceedingly heavy, and exceedingly hard, though it is rather less hard on quarrying than it becomes a few months later. Ancient ships were small, ancient land-transport primitive. A finished statue weighs about half the original block. It is therefore possible that some of the roughing-out of the sculpture was done near the quarries: this is nothing but a guess, and there may have been some method, unknown to us, of transporting the blocks on rafts; it would also mean that the force of craftsmen was at times divided between the Cyclades and the Peloponnese, and that would create other difficulties; but it remains a possibility.

Marble carving is a laborious, lengthy process, and exhausting in the sense that a sculptor cannot work more than a limited number of hours a day. Modern sculptors estimate that it would take one man, working steadily and continuously, about a year to carve a single life-size statue in Parian marble. There are some twenty figures in each pediment, all larger than life, and those towards the centre considerably larger; and it should be remembered that a figure twice life-size has four times the area to carve. There were in addition twelve metopes, each with two or sometimes three figures almost life-size, in very high relief. All these sculptures were completed, from quarry to final position, within a dozen years.

The inference is clear: a number of carvers must have been employed. How were they organized? Here again we are almost completely in the dark. There must have been someone, whether one man or a committee, who chose the subjects, or at least approved them when chosen; but there cannot have been more than one man to prepare the main design of each pediment and each metope. Tradition, as we have seen, names two main artists, one for each pediment, and this seems not unlikely. The same two may have divided the designs of the metopes between them, or may have delegated them to others; but since the same spirit reigns throughout, the team of designers, if it was a team, must have been closely knit.

We have been talking of design. Execution is a different matter, for here assistants were essential, and because the style is so consistent we must assume that these assistants were highly trained and carefully supervised. Within the general uniformity there are, of course, differences of touch, but the general effect is completely harmonious. There cannot have been much difference of date between the various sculptures, since the overall limits of time were too small: so that, if we speak of one part being earlier or later in style than another, this must mean that one designer or sculptor was more old-fashioned than another.

The original designs may have been in the form of drawings, but at quite an early stage they must have been translated into three dimensions, in other words into models in wax or clay on a fairly large scale. This was essential for several reasons. Only in this way could the designer work out in detail the three-dimensional composition, which in the interlocked groups of the west pediment is often highly complex. Only in this way could he determine what degree of relief he was to give them, how much marble could be safely cut away without endangering the stability of the figure or group, and how they were to fit into the none too easy field. Finally, this method, combined with personal supervision of all stages of the carving of the marble blocks, would be far the most efficient way of indicating to his assistants what he was wanting them to produce. Being a working sculptor he no doubt did some of the carving himself: we cannot say how much or at what stages, but a little thought will show which are the most critical, and when he is most likely to have intervened. There must also have been some system of transferring at least the major measurements of the models to the marble blocks as they were being worked, but we do not know how elaborate this was, or how close it came to the modern system of 'pointing'.

The method of preparing models in wax or clay encourages more movement both laterally and in depth than does direct carving into a rectangular marble block, which imposes a strong degree of frontality. This may partly account for the remarkable freedom of composition in many of the figures, as well as for other features hitherto unknown in Greek sculpture; and these we must now consider.

GENERAL CHARACTER. In the history of art the general character of these sculptures is of peculiar interest. The second quarter of the fifth century B.C., called today the Early Classical period, saw the break-up of many of the archaic conventions. Old types of statues were abandoned; and old ways of stylizing drapery, hair, and muscles, which had sometimes become stereotyped and empty of their original meaning at the end of the archaic period, now yielded to a more experimental phase. Archaic sculptors had been great lovers of pattern, and although the tendency to create pattern is never absent from art, at this time, and notably in the sculptures of this temple, that tendency was subordinate to the direct study and rendering of natural appearances. Sculptors suddenly realized that they had at their command the means of expressing what had rarely and never consistently been expressed in sculpture before. They looked with fresh eyes and saw a new world, apparently within their reach, in which men could be shown as they really were; and this knowledge led to further observation and further discovery. The history of art shows that such attempts to capture complete reality are often

Fig. 1. View eastwards up the valley of the Alpheios. The Hill of Kronos is at the left, with the Altis at its foot.
In the foreground the gorge of the Kladeos and, on the right (just outside the picture), its junction with the Alpheios.

Fig. 2. Remains of the Temple of Zeus, from the North.

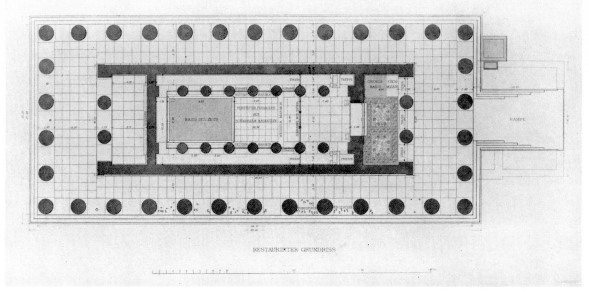

Fig. 3. Reconstruction of the ground plan of the Temple, after Dörpfeld.

Fig. 4. Reconstruction of the East front, after Dörpfeld.

Fig. 5. Reconstruction of the elevation of the pronaos, after Dörpfeld.

Fig. 6. Model of the Altis, second century A.D., from the South-west. Olympia, Museum.

Fig. 7. Lion's head gutter-spout from the Temple of Zeus.
Fifth century B.C. Olympia, Museum.

Fig. 8. Lion's head gutter-spout from the Temple of Zeus.
Fifth century B.C. Olympia, Museum.

Fig. 9. Lion's head gutter-spout from the Temple of Zeus.
Fourth century B.C. Olympia, Museum.

Fig. 10. Lion's head gutter-spout from the Temple of Zeus.
First century B.C. Olympia, Museum.

Fig. 11. Silver coin of Arkadia, fourth century B.C., from a cast. Enlarged.
Obverse: Head of Dionysus. Reverse: The young Arkas.

Fig. 12. Bronze coin of Hadrian, A.D. 133, perhaps showing
the head of the statue of Zeus by Pheidias. Berlin. Actual size.

Fig. 13. Bronze coin of Hadrian, A.D. 137, perhaps showing
the statue of Zeus by Pheidias.
Florence, Archaeological Museum. Actual size. From a cast.

Fig. 14. Model of the East pediment, arrangement proposed by B. Ashmole.

Fig. 15. Model of the East pediment, arrangement proposed by N. Yalouris.

Fig. 16. Model of the West pediment as in the fifth century B.C.

Fig. 17. Model of the West pediment as in the first century B.C.

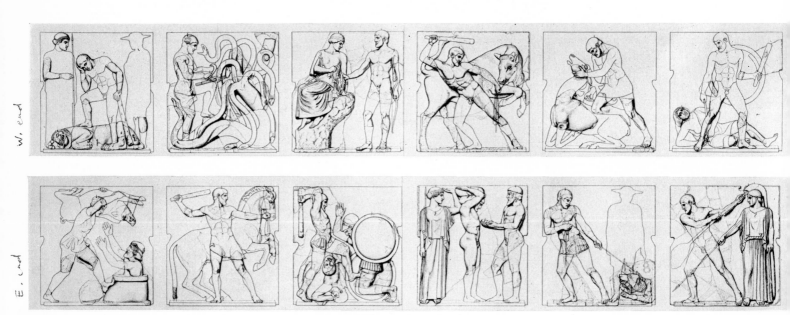

Fig. 18. Drawing of the metopes, by Max Kühnert, from Curtius and Adler, *Olympia*, III, pl. xlv. For later changes and additions see pp. 181 ff.

the pursuit of a mirage; but it also shows that, clumsy though they may sometimes be, they are in themselves an achievement, and possess a quality often absent in more accomplished work.

In the sculpture of this temple they may be seen everywhere: they seek to express, in the drapery, the weight of the stuff and the way in which this causes it to hang, to fold when girded, to swing and crumple when in motion: in the bodies, volume and solidity, the differences between bone and muscle, between muscles tense and slack, and the effects of a movement on the whole organism: in the hair, its weight, flow, and texture: in the faces, a reflection of the mood. Emotion is distilled to its essence and expressed in the line of a nostril, the stiffening of a lip, or in the set of the eyes; and it is worth remembering that this is the first time in European sculpture, except perhaps for the archaic smile, which is in rather a different category, that the attempt had ever been made to show emotion in the face.

Parallel with the heightened interest in the nature and appearance of body and drapery, and made possible by increasing command of the medium, were two other advances: a wider range of individual subjects, and a freedom to choose for presentation the moment in a story different from that which had attracted archaic artists. The repertory now includes youth, maturity, and age, and can indicate their physical and psychological differences; and whereas an archaic artist liked to depict the climax of an action, the early classical artist tends to choose the moment before, when the tension is mounting, or the moment after, when the tension is gone and the consequences appear. He can now show by subtlety of pose and expression not only the emotional state of individuals but their emotional relationship to one another.

POSTURE AND GESTURE. One other factor must always be remembered in studying ancient art, the importance of the poise of the head, the posture of the body and limbs, and the gestures of the hands. In ancient times there was a whole language of gesture and posture which is almost lost to us today, though in the south of Europe its relics survive. In antiquity this language must have been universally understood, and it had a certain standard vocabulary which people came to know partly through everyday conversation accompanied by gestures, partly through the movements and poses of dancing, which formed an important part of Greek life and education; and partly through the drama, because the movements of the actors and of the chorus, in their masks and heavy formal clothing, had to be strongly stylized. It resembled and was perhaps one of the ancestors of the silent, even more elaborate and subtle language of dancing and drama in Asia, which still possesses a large repertory of poses and gestures, each of which has its own special clearly differentiated meaning. To the ancient public these things, fixed in the memory by pictorial and sculptural art, were common knowledge: we must try to recognize and interpret them if we are to understand the sculptures fully.

THE PEDIMENTS

In the original publication of the sculptures (*Olympia*, vol. III), Georg Treu arranged the figures in each pediment in what he considered to be the correct order, and then lettered them from left to right alphabetically. It is convenient to use these letters, even where the arrangement implied by them is no longer accepted. Many arrangements have been suggested, especially for the east pediment: a conspectus of them, with diagrams, is given by G. Becatti, *Il Maestro di Olimpia* (1943), but no final solution has been reached. The arrangement proposed below (p. 13) is that of S. Stucchi, based on the series of careful observations recorded by him in vol. XIV–XVI (N.S.), 1952–54, of the *Annuario* of the Italian School of Archaeology in Athens; but it involves, as will be seen, two serious difficulties (p. 16). Dr. Yalouris (p. 173 ff) has a far different arrangement, which avoids these, but is not free from others of its own.

THE EAST PEDIMENT
(Plates 1–61 and folding plate at the end of the book)

SUBJECT. The subject of the east pediment was eminently suitable for the heart of the sanctuary: it was the preparation for the chariot-race by which Pelops made himself master of Elis against Oinomaos of Pisa, and it provided a legendary parallel to the ousting of the Pisatans from the control of the festival and their complete subjugation, which had just been accomplished. The race had begun at the altar of Zeus at Olympia; Zeus had presided; and it must have been regarded as the first of the chariot-races that were perhaps the most spectacular event in the Festival, and certainly that in which a victory was most highly prized.

The legend was sinister, and its echoes are heard throughout Greek literature. Oinomaos, king of Pisa, had an only daughter Hippodameia, and had received an oracle that he would die at the hands of his son-in-law. He devised a formidable safeguard: anyone who came as her suitor had to compete with him in a chariot-race from the river Kladeos at Olympia to the altar of Poseidon on the isthmus of Corinth. The suitor started first, taking Hippodameia with him. Oinomaos sacrificed a ram to Zeus and then set off in pursuit: if he overtook the suitor he speared him to death. Since the horses of Oinomaos were divine it seemed that the issue could not be in doubt, and thirteen suitors had already perished in this way when Pelops, according to most accounts a foreigner from Phrygia or Lydia, arrived and claimed the hand of Hippodameia. There is more than one version of the way in which he succeeded in obtaining it. The simpler version is that told by Pindar in his first Olympian Ode: Pelops had prayed to Poseidon, who loved him, and had been given horses swifter even than those of Oinomaos. But this does not explain how or why Oinomaos was killed; and the more logical and more picturesque version is that Pelops had bribed Myrtilos, the charioteer of Oinomaos, to substitute lynch-pins of wax for the metal lynch-pins of his chariot: the wheels came off, Oinomaos

12

was thrown and killed, and Pelops took his daughter and his kingdom. There was a terrible sequel. In order to avoid paying Myrtilos the promised bribe, which according to one account was no less than the favours of his newly-won bride, Pelops is said to have made away with Myrtilos by drowning him. Myrtilos, in dying, cursed him and his whole race: the curse brought fearful evils on his sons Atreus and Thyestes, and on their sons too; and the tragedies that haunted Atreus and the ruling house of Mycenae – the sacrifice of Iphigeneia, the murder of Agamemnon, the killing of his mother Klytaimnestra by Orestes, were familiar to everyone through literature and drama. But not everyone realized, until they stood before the temple and saw high above them this vivid scene, that the origins of that series of tragedies lay here in Olympia, in the plot that was coming to fruition at that moment, when the chariots were being led out and the two competitors were trusting, one to his invincible horses, the other to his simple but deadly subterfuge.

ARRANGEMENT OF THE FIGURES (figs. 14-15). The place where the race starts is shown by the presence of the river-gods Alpheios (A) and Kladeos (P) in the south and north angles of 1-12 the pediment: as we have seen, the Alpheios flows near the southern boundary of the site, whilst the Kladeos flows from north to south and joins the Alpheios not far from the south-west corner. Kladeos is shown as a young man of great physical but no obvious intellectual power: Alpheios as more mature and heavily built. It seems improbable that a river-god so widely revered as the Alpheios would have been beardless, and the fragment of marble within his hand may well be the end of his beard, which, as can be seen in other figures on the pediment, does not necessarily touch the throat.

To turn now to the main scene. In the centre is Zeus (H): in his left hand, originally, a thunder- 13-14 bolt. Before the race a sacrifice was made on the altar of Zeus, and Pausanias, thinking perhaps of a sacrifice as being offered before a statue, calls this central figure a statue. There is nothing to indicate that this was the intention of the sculptor, and it is better to regard it as a living presence, invisible to the competitors. Although the head is missing, the muscles of the neck show that it was inclined towards Pelops (G), who stands on his right (our left), the side of good 49 omen. But there is a terrible irony in this. The victory of Pelops gave him the kingdom of Olympia, but it brought in its train to one generation after another a whole series of disasters. Originally Pelops was shown as young and rather slender, in heroic nudity except for his helmet. At some later date, possibly three centuries or so after the temple was built, when 46, 47 repairs or reconstruction were necessary, this figure was furnished with a bronze cuirass and a bronze helmet, which was fitted on over the marble one.

On the other side of Zeus is Oinomaos (I), and whether Zeus is visible to him or not, his 15, 18, 20 dropped jaw, with open mouth, seems to show that he realizes the omens are against him.

We may reasonably assume that the figures on Pelops' side of the pediment are his retinue, whilst those on the other comprise the household of Oinomaos. Accordingly we ought to place beside Oinomaos his wife Sterope (F), and although the figure is fragmentary there is 48, 45

no doubt about her identity: the small fragment of the head is covered with hair of a peculiar
character; its texture and the way in which it is combed forward show that it is both sparse and
wispy, as commonly in old age. She wears the simple form of Doric peplos without a girdle:
it is a kind of dress suitable for wearing in the house and allows one to see that her figure is
slack and heavy. Her gesture, which can be reconstructed from the fragments, is an index of
her thoughts: she rests her left elbow in her right hand with the left hand raised to the chin, a
recognized sign of anxiety or grief. Her daughter Hippodameia (K), who should stand on the
far side of Pelops, wears a more serviceable kind of dress, the Doric peplos with a girdle, and
her body is slenderer than her mother's, firmer and more compact. She too makes an apposite
movement, raising her left hand to her neck. This can be interpreted in one of two ways,
perhaps in both. She is wearing a veil on her shoulders and the veil in antiquity was the symbol
of the bride, just as it is today: but she is fastening or adjusting it, and this may be a hint of her
preparation for the journey she is about to take beside Pelops: to ride at speed in an ancient
chariot, which was springless, must have been both rough and strenuous.

In the chariot-teams (D, M) the designer encountered one of his main physical difficulties:
the pediment was far too shallow to accommodate four hourses harnessed abreast. Archaic
sculptors, one even as late as the Alkmeonid pediment at Delphi, faced with a similar problem
not much more than a generation before Olympia, tried to solve it by presenting the horses in
frontal view, with heads, chests, and forelegs showing, their bodies grossly foreshortened,
and the chariot with its occupants behind them, in an unnaturally close plane. The designer
here has thought out a better solution: the chariot-team is set sideways to the spectator, and
the near horse is almost in the round, free of and slightly behind the others, which are in high
relief. This arrangement economizes space and corresponds neatly with reality, because in an
ancient chariot the trace-horses were less closely harnessed than the pole-horses. The chariots
themselves were probably of bronze, appropriately foreshortened and, like the teams, were
perhaps set rather differently from one another, since the chariot of Pelops (D) was wheeling
into position, whilst that of Oinomaos (M) was still at rest, because, by the terms of the
contest, he started later than the suitor.

We now turn to one of the most impressive figures in either pediment, the old man (N)
seated on the ground behind the chariot of Oinomaos. His position is certain, partly because he
is carved to be seen from his left side, partly because the slope of the pediment and the position
of the horses prevents him from being moved more than a few inches one way or the other.
Again the attitude is full of meaning. The hand is raised towards the mouth – still an instinctive
movement of dismay – and the gaze is directed towards the centre. The anxiety that pervades
him is seen in the intent eyes, the parted lips, the sensitive nostrils, and the lined and contracted forehead; whilst age shows in the thinning hair, the sagging lower eyelid, the deep
line from the nostril, and the closely-observed fleshy torso. A good deal of detail was left to the
painter, especially in the beard, the moustache, and the top of the head, but the sculptor has
been careful to stress the play of shadow on the fringe of the hair and the end of the beard by

44, 48

16, 17
19, 21

53-54,
28-30

53
30

31-40

marking the spiral ends of the carefully-articulated locks with a central drill-hole. Two other technical details may be noted. One is the displacement of the head on the torso in order that the view of the figure as it was set in the pediment might be satisfactory: the other is the linear   37
detail, in the shape of smaller folds, which has been carved on that part of the drapery over the hips which could be seen from the front. If this is original and not a later touching-up, it shows how much was given by the models (the drapery out of sight seems more basic) and how much   40
could be added when it came to the actual carving. Altogether this is a powerful but restrained study of age and emotion such as had not been seen in Europe before; but the anxious seer as a tragic character was already traditional, for he appears on several painted vases, which were perhaps all inspired by some major work of art, nearly a century earlier: in these the seer is also seated on the ground, and can be recognized by his attitude of grief, as his master Amphiaraos departs to join the disastrous expedition of the Seven against Thebes. On the finest of these vases, a mixing-bowl of Corinthian make (fig. 19), the name of the seer is Hali-medes, and the seer at Olympia can also be named, though not with certainty, as Iamos. Iamos was the son of Apollo: wishing to learn his destiny he went down into the bed of the Alpheios, and after bathing in its waters was directed by Apollo to Olympia, and was given the power to foretell the future from the sacrifices on the altar of Zeus. Although no altar is shown, we may either assume that that is where his gaze is now fixed; or we may prefer to think that he is no longer looking at the altar, but into the ominous future.

On Pelops' side of the pediment is another elderly man (L). He too must be a seer, and   58-61
although his features are lined he has not the anxious look of his counterpart: the figure is much mutilated, but a newly-added fragment establishes the poise of the head, which is raised, and is turning towards the centre as if he too were receiving some sign of the outcome of the contest. He wears a curious un-Greek headdress, a cloth covering the top of the head: this may be intended to remind us that Pelops came from overseas, with foreigners in his train. His position in the pediment is fixed: not only does his height limit him to a certain area, but the marble of the back of his head is cut away to produce a flat inclined surface which must have fitted the raking ceiling of the pediment.

So far the arrangement is tolerably certain, but the difficulties now begin when we come to consider the four remaining figures (C, B, O, E), for these are to some extent interchangeable; and the difficulties are not lessened by Pausanias having described them all as male, whereas one is certainly female. Some help is to be had from the size of the figures and from their poses, since the size of some of them precludes their being placed too far out towards the corners; and they are made to be seen only from certain points of view.

We begin with the barefoot kneeling girl (O). Only two positions seem possible, since she   22-27
is carved so as to be seen from her left side, and this means that in order not to be facing away from the central group she must be on our right of the pediment. She has sometimes been placed in front of the horses of Oinomaos, in which case she would presumably be a handmaid of Sterope or Hippodameia. But Pausanias does state that the person at the head of the horses

was Myrtilos the charioteer, which suggests that he was in some way busied with them, perhaps holding the bridles. It is possible that Pausanias mistook the girl's dress for the customary long dress of a male charioteer; but if he did, and if she was indeed in front of the horses' heads, where is Myrtilos? In any case, someone must have been in control of the horses, and the seer (N) clearly was not. If on the other hand we set her in the only other place available, behind the seer of Oinomaos (N), she would displace the crouching boy (E), and E was found in front

41-43 of the first intercolumniation of the temple from its north end, apparently as if he had fallen from this very place in the pediment. Dr. Yalouris (p. 176) thinks that E should be in this place, and has an interesting explanation of his identity, but his arrangement too is not without difficulties. This is a dilemma which has so far not been resolved. We tentatively place the girl (O) behind the seer of Oinomaos, but the objection to this is that the outside of her right thigh is tooled away as if to fit it against another figure. The possible positions for E and for the naked kneeling youth (B) are then narrowed down to two: one under the heads of Oinomaos' horses, the other under those of Pelops, because the other vacant position immediately behind the horses of Pelops must be assigned to the kneeling man with a cloak round his lower limbs (C). His arms were in front of him, and his chest-muscles are contracted as if he were

55-57 holding the reins: he is the charioteer of Pelops, whose name was Sphairos, or as the guide told Pausanias, Killas; and his size, his function, and the fact that he is made to be seen from his right, locate him here: he is not on this occasion going to drive the chariot, nor is he suitably dressed to do so.

Now one character is missing from Oinomaos' side of the pediment, his charioteer Myrtilos who, even if he was not so closely involved in the plot as some versions of the legend affirm,

50-52 was an essential figure. It has been suggested that he is the naked kneeling youth (B), and that he knelt in front of Oinomaos' team, almost facing the front, with his right hand crossing his chest and passing up the left side of his face apparently to hold the reins or a bridle. The objection to this identification is that the youth is shown by the forms of his body and the absence of hair upon it to be little more than a boy, and if we accept this arrangement we must assume that the sculptor had in mind not the version of the story which tells how the race was won by the bribing of Myrtilos, but that in which there was no treachery, and Pelops' victory was gained by means of the team of horses given him by Poseidon.

This leaves one place vacant, under the heads of the other chariot-team, that of Pelops, and

41-43 here could be set the one remaining figure, the young seated boy (E) who was facing the front, with his head, now missing, slightly turned to his left. He has been leading up the team from the stable where it had been harnessed, and now, his task over, he sits with his hands idle and his whole body relaxed. The subject is one of the most difficult for sculptors: here, the problems of pose and foreshortening inseparable from it are admirably solved. The cloak is used to encase the body almost like the shell of a nut, and to provide a compact silhouette. This is yet another example of the pioneering temper of these sculptors: not only is the composition and the use of clothing to consolidate it new, but the study of the youthful body with its tender unmuscular flesh has a freshness which distinguishes it from the conventions both of the archaic and of the classical age. It is true that the next, fully classical generation was to reap the advantage of these experiments in realism and to subsume them into its own deliberately ideal style, but experiment itself was cut short then, and was never taken up again with the same un-self-conscious directness. Hellenistic realism is a very different matter, and cannot forget its classical past.

THE WEST PEDIMENT
(Plates 62-142 and folding plate at the end of the book)

SUBJECT. The main lines of composition in the east pediment are the five heavy verticals in the centre, the long horizontal bodies of the horses meeting these, and sloping or reclining figures filling the corners. Quiet poses, tense excitement. In the west pediment, by contrast, it seems that everything is tumult, a series of violent undulations stabilized only by the great vertical central figure with the outstretched arm (L). The occasion was the wedding feast of Peirithoos. Peirithoos, king of a northern Greek tribe, the Lapiths, was marrying Deidameia. He could hardly omit to invite his nearest neighbours, the centaurs, a tribe so wild, so northerly, that they were half man, half horse. All went well at the feast until the centaurs had had too much wine, and then, their bestial instincts getting the upper hand, they suddenly attacked the women and boys and tried to carry them off. The scene is appropriate to the temple of Zeus in that Peirithoos was a grandson of Zeus; but its deeper significance lay in the presence of Apollo (L), the son of Zeus, patron of all the arts, and of all that makes life humane and decent. His presence ensures that civilized man shall prevail. As with Zeus in the east pediment, we must think of Apollo as a spiritual presence invisible to the combatants: he takes no physical part in the fight, but sways it by his imperious gesture, by his stern but calm expression and by the slight downward inclination of the head which strengthens the direction of the eyes.

101–109

But here there is an unexpected difficulty. Pausanias does not mention Apollo, and calls the central figure Peirithoos. Now it is true that Peirithoos was partly divine, being in fact the grandson of Zeus, but this would hardly entitle him to be placed in the centre of a pediment of the temple of Zeus, as counterpart to the figure of Zeus himself in the other pediment, and in a position which the example of late archaic temples shows was now always reserved for an Olympian god. There are other objections too: Peirithoos was in legend the close friend of Theseus, who was himself the son of one of the greatest of the Olympians, Poseidon. Theseus is present here (M); yet if Pausanias is right, he is shown on a grotesquely smaller scale than the friend by whose side he is fighting. Further, the central figure stands apart from and above the conflict, and none of the participants seems aware of him. One last point, he was holding in his left hand an object which is shown by the socket in which it fitted to have been a bow: the bow is above all things the weapon of Apollo, and even if Peirithoos was holding one on this occasion – and it is difficult to see why he should choose this particular weapon, or how he came

92–97

by it – he would surely be using it to rescue his bride who is being assaulted before his eyes at his own wedding feast. One or two modern scholars have attempted to justify Pausanias' identification, but it must surely be wrong. Whether his guide misled him, whether, when the guide pointed up to the pediment and mentioned Peirithoos, Pausanias assumed that he was pointing to the central figure, or whether Pausanias misread his own notes later, we shall never know.

Accepting as we must, then, the central figure as Apollo, we are forced to the conclusion that a picturesque character often present on this occasion has been either omitted or given a subordinate position. This is Kaineus, who, having been made invulnerable by Poseidon, could only be overcome by the centaurs piling rocks upon him until he was buried in the earth. It may well be that the designer could not work this cumbrous incident into his composition, and so decided to omit it. Kaineus is not essential to the story, as Theseus is, and may not be present at all; or he may be one of the Lapiths further away from the centre and not specially characterized.

ARRANGEMENT OF THE FIGURES (figs. 16-17). The wild scene looks chaotic only at first glance: when the composition is analysed it is found to be strongly even if not rigidly symmetrical, and controlled by a careful rhythm of decreasing momentum from the centre to the corners. We have again a main group consisting of the god in the centre with two heroes, one on each side of him, each striking outwards at a centaur who is attacking a woman. Again, as in the east pediment, the use of an equine body to ease the transition between the huge upright figures in the centre and the smaller ones in the narrowing field.

Thus the main composition: but although some elements are fixed with certainty there has been much argument about the position of some of the others. Indeed a doubt arises even with the two main groups, each of a centaur attacking a woman (H, I, N, O).

110-117   As at present exhibited in the museum, Eurytion (I), the centaur who has seized the bride (H), is placed on the spectator's right of Apollo; and the centaur (N) with the bride's com-
98-100   panion (O), the nympheutria or, as we should say, the lady of honour, on our left; and the two heroes, Peirithoos and Theseus, strike inwards at the two monsters. In this way bride and bridegroom are ignored by Apollo, whose outstretched arm is directed away from them towards the group with Theseus, which, in the story, must necessarily be second in importance. If these two groups are interchanged, bringing the bride and her attacker across to our left side of the pediment, it will be necessary to set Peirithoos and Theseus in such a way that they are striking outwards each from one side of Apollo, and not, as at present, towards the centre.
118-121   The figure of Peirithoos is in fragments and even the head is much defaced. The head of the
112-114   bride is, however, perfectly preserved, and it is interesting to see how little to the modern eye she is affected by what is taking place. The main reason for this is the ideal of how a Greek of heroic strain, whether man or woman, should behave in such a situation: a second is that the tendency towards the observation and record of natural detail which we have remarked in

the bodies and drapery (and, with the seer of the east pediment, also in the face), never approaches exact imitation: it is always transmuted in the sculptor's mind, and given the stamp of his style, which is part traditional and only part individual.

A third reason is that this direct approach to nature is new and tentative, and, as the subsequent history of Greek sculpture shows, soon to be submerged in the all-pervading classic ideal. Accordingly, on the face of the bride there is no trace of pain or terror, only a calm determination – shown in the fixed gaze, the set of the nostril, and the line of the mouth – to free herself from the grip of the hands which clutch her breast and waist, and the foreleg which   110-111 is curled round behind her. She thrusts her left elbow against her attacker's jaw, forcing his head aside and causing him to wince with the pain, as his lips and nostrils show. The centaur   92 who has seized the bride's companion is equally discomfited: although he holds her between   98-100 his forelegs she resists vigorously, grasping his beard and his ear and pushing his head upwards so that his human body is bent backwards. He flings out an arm behind him, perhaps to ward off the blow from Theseus, who comes in from the rear. The centaur's horse-body is in fine   92 trim and the muscles ripple as he leaps forward. This contrasts with the bride's attacker, whose lean and leathery hindquarters suggest that he is older and out of condition.

On the outer sides of this central complex of seven figures – the god, and on each side of him a hero attacking a centaur who is assaulting a woman – are two groups of two figures each. The subject is similar but not identical in both: in one (P, Q) a centaur is locked in a struggle   82-91 with a youth, in the other (F, G) a centaur is attempting to carry off a younger boy. Their size   122-126 and shape establish their position at a certain point in the pediment where the ceiling is still high enough for them to go in: the question is which went on which side. Their present arrangement is unlikely to be right, and it is better to reverse them, placing the youth and centaur on our right of the pediment and the boy and centaur on our left.

Its inherent probability made the attack on a young boy by a centaur a regular feature of the story: it recurs on a metope of the Parthenon shortly after this, and on the frieze of the temple at Phigaleia a generation later. On the other hand the episode of the centaur biting the youth, though plausible in the circumstances, seems to be unique in sculpture; but it is carefully thought out and depicted with dramatic force: the centaur buries his teeth in the arm of the youth,   82, 86 who does not let go but grins with the pain. Indeed, he cannot let go, for the arm with which he had encircled the centaur's neck has been held with both hands: one grips the biceps, the other grips the hand. This is the fiercest of the fights: the wild and shaggy centaur snarls like the animal he is, and the eyes, nostrils, and forehead are heavily, almost grotesquely lined. The youth's forehead too is lined, the nostril distended and sharply furrowed where it adjoins the cheek, the mouth open and distorted with pain: even the eyelids, and the eyeballs with   90 their axes of sight converging, add to the effect. In fact, the sculptor has gone so far as to carve the eyeballs into angular instead of spherical contours in order to intensify their expression.

The designer has not included the whole body of the centaur: since it was in three-quarter view, that would have been impossible from lack of space. Thus, althouhg it has no background, the group is a high relief and not completed behind. Perhaps because of its not being designed fully in the round, and because of some mistake in the model or in the copying, the youth's **85, 86** left leg is far from satisfactory. The designer must have intended it to be bent at the knee, with the lower leg extended backwards: but this is not the impression created; the knee is not sufficiently defined, and the thigh appears to be prolonged downwards and to merge into a pillar-like mass of drapery.

One more technical point: there is an uncarved patch in the hair above the centre of the **90** youth's forehead which may have something to do with the method of copying. This point was sometimes used as a datum-point in laying out a system of measurements (for instance in Egyptian sculpture) and it is possible that as such it was isolated at an early stage in the carving and left as a fixed point until the last: then, for some reason, perhaps because there was too little marble for carving a curl, it was never finished. There are analogous areas on the heads **58-61** of one or two of the other figures, for instance the seer of Pelops in the east pediment, and **147-148** Athena in the metope of the lion.

122-126 Little is left of the group which balanced this, a centaur trying to carry off a boy (F, G); but enough remains to show that the sculptor studied the characteristic forms of youth with care, and produced a slender torso in which the structure of the bones is lightly but surely indicated through the thin covering of flesh and undeveloped muscle.

Further from the centre, and located exactly by their shape and size, come two groups each consisting of three figures, a centaur attacking a girl but at the same time being attacked by **71-81,** a Lapith (C, D, E: R, S, T). Though not exactly alike, they balance each other closely in subject **127-142** and design. This is extremely complicated, and here particularly one feels that models rather than drawings must have been produced by the master-designer for his assistants to work from. The shallowness of the pediment again made it impossible to create the centaurs completely in the round, and their horse-bodies are considerably flattened; but from the front they present a convincing picture: they are down on their chests, but their hindlegs are upright, so that the horse-bodies are bent at a perilous angle until the backs look as if they were near breaking-point. In both groups stability is given to this unwieldy mass of marble by carving the girl's body in one piece with the centaur's.

In the main composition these groups are an important factor, since although their lines carry on the undulating rhythm which runs from the centre out into the corners of the pediment, the action within each group is almost in equilibrium, and in each the powerful body of the Lapith, thrusting inwards, serves to buttress the whole central scene and to focus instead of dissipating its interest.

Within the same basic formula the sculptor has nicely differentiated the action and the actors: one of the centaurs (S) seizes his victim by waist and foot, the other his by the hair; and his other hand being occupied in keeping himself from collapse, he contrives to plant a **71, 72** hoof upon her thigh. One of the Lapiths (C) flings the whole weight of his body into the attack, **127** the other (T) kneels, and uses a knife. In both groups the hands are expressive: those of the centaurs contrasting with soft flesh and fine strands of hair, those of the girls thrusting away the coarse head or trying to detach the monstrous hand.

In the group on the left (C, D, E) the Lapith is pulling down the centaur, holding him by the head and shoulders, and the centaur uses his right arm to save himself. His left hand grasps the girl's long hair: the mechanism of the grip and the forms which it creates have been well understood: bone, flesh, veins, and tendons are minutely studied and faithfully characterized. Nor is the rest of the body neglected: the sculptor has shirked none of its anatomical difficulties, and has made a remarkably convincing attempt to incorporate a human navel in an equine chest. The head is more strongly stylized, as if it had never received the final realistic touches: there are harsh double wrinkles above the nostril, and one equally harsh from nostril to mouth: the modelling and wrinkling of forehead and brows is pattern-like, but there is a curious touch of attempted realism on the right temple: where the Lapith's arm passed, a tuft of hair is reversed in direction and the locks spray upwards, but the roots come too low on the forehead. *71-81* *79* *76* *77*

The girl's pose is much contorted: her left arm must have been raised towards her head, but the right arm is stretched out backwards and thrusts away the head of the centaur, holding it by the ear. Her own face was most sensitive, and, battered though it is, the delicate modelling round the eyes and nose and mouth still tells: the hair is exquisite too, but judged as a piece of realism it stops short too sharply on the temples and fails to suggest that it is rooted on the scalp. *73, 81*

In the group on the right (R, S, T) the centaur has seized the girl by her left ankle with his left hand and with the other hand has torn off the dress from her left breast: she grasps this hand in both of hers and strives to detach it. This subject, never before attempted, has led the sculptor to make a thorough-going study, for instance of the loosened mass in the middle, with its superimposed groups of folds; of the collapsing folds round the right knee where they strike the ground; and of the reeded folds over the left leg where the centaur twists and pulls: all these have a strongly realistic origin but are treated with an agreeable touch of formal style. In the body, the poise of the head is eloquent, as are the slenderness of the arms, and the tender, youthful breast. The centaur is perhaps less successful, the curve of his back too improbable, and the modelling of his chest lacking in interest: but the great mat of the beard is impressive, and one would gladly know what the head was like that went with it. The girl's body provides a foil to the muscular torso of the Lapith (T), who lunges forward and thrusts a long knife (perhaps a sacrificial knife, and the only weapon in the scene except the bow of Apollo) through the right breast of the centaur: the point emerged at the top of the shoulder and was made of bronze, as was the lower part of the blade near the Lapith's hand. It is thought that these were added in Hellenistic times when additions in metal were made elsewhere: Pelops, for instance, in the east pediment, was given bronze armour and the centaur Eurytion, in the west, a large bronze wreath. *127-142* *132-133* *142* *130-131* *136* *137* *139, 142*

The four corner figures (A, B, U, V) present a number of problems. We begin with that in the extreme southern angle of the pediment (V). It is headless, but the subject can be identified: *62-70* *65, 70* a heavily-built woman, a serving-woman perhaps, lying prone, her breasts exposed, clutching her dress on her left shoulder: it has been torn from her body when she was attacked: now she has escaped, and from some hiding-place is watching the outcome of the struggle. Her right arm is carved, not in the Parian marble used by the original sculptors, but in Pentelic, and is an ancient restoration, probably of the second century B.C. So much is clear. The figure in

62-63 the northern corner (A), whose position corresponds and whose action is similar, is carved entirely in Pentelic marble, and is therefore a replacement of the original, which must have been so much damaged that it could not be repaired. The restorer has tried to copy the original composition, and this northern figure is almost a reversed replica of the southern, but later

64, 66, elements of style can easily be detected in the details. The remaining two figures (B, U), one
67-69 on each side of the pediment and both of elderly women, are also of Pentelic marble. Are they replacements for originals so much damaged that they could not be repaired, or are they entirely new additions made after a severe earthquake or fire, when extensive reconstruction was unavoidable, and it was felt that this was an opportunity to remedy what seemed a defect to the florid taste of middle Hellenistic times, the sparse filling of the pediment? This has been strongly argued, and it has been suggested that this was the same occasion when the various embellishments in bronze were added, which would have a similar effect in making the pedimental figures seem less meagre. Also in favour of this view is the raising of the figures on

66 cushions (the cushion of the old woman on our right (U) is made of a recut fragment of the earlier and now lost figure in the northern corner); since elsewhere in both pediments the figures are on even ground and in full view, whereas these two were difficult to see. At some time, too, the other figures in the pediment have been trimmed and pushed closer together than they were originally as if to make room for extra figures. If we accept these arguments,

67 we have to explain what was the model for the head of the old woman (B) which, despite its obviously later technique and some anachronisms in its style, certainly seems to hark back to a sculpture of the same date as the temple. A possible answer is that the figure in the southern

65 angle (V) was elderly, and that her head, now lost, served as the model. The head of the old
68 woman next but one to the southern corner (U) looks more like a pure Hellenistic creation. (On the date of these figures see also p. 179.)

THE METOPES
Plates 143-211

SUBJECTS. The decision to provide twelve metopes and to fill them with the Labours of Herakles could not have been bettered. Herakles was the son of Zeus and the great-grandson of Pelops; he was the founder of the Olympic Games, and had himself marked out the boundaries of the Altis. He was the exemplar of what an athlete should be – self-disciplined, determined, and courageous. He was almost a local hero: many of his deeds had been performed in the Peloponnese, and one, the cleaning of the stables of King Augeias, on this very spot.

His main deeds, called not very happily 'Labours', after the Roman word, had become canonical by the time the temple was built: that is to say it was generally agreed which were those that had been performed under Eurystheus, king of Tiryns, during the twelve years when Herakles served him at the command of the Delphic Oracle. But most of the deeds had been current in story long before this, and it would be interesting to know what sources the designer used. There must have been traditional versions preserved by the poets, whether in the written word or in their songs. Pindar, for instance, when about the same time he wrote odes in honour of Olympic victors, obviously had access to such sources; and where the myth was local, for instance the contest of Oinomaos in the east pediment, or the Augean stables in the metope, there may have been a local tradition still current. In short, the stories were well known by word of mouth. But in addition to the poetic and folk traditions there was also a pictorial tradition, partly dependent upon them. Hundreds of Peloponnesian vases must once have existed, especially those made in Corinth and Laconia, on which these deeds were depicted. There are still hundreds of such pictures on Athenian vases, and there must originally have been thousands. There were also relief-sculptures: some of these have survived, and they too must have existed in larger numbers than at present. With so much repetition it was inevitable that compositions should become stereotyped, and in some of the metopes at Olympia, for example that of the Erymanthian boar, where Eurystheus has taken refuge in a storage-jar and the animal is deposited on top of him, the designer – to assume for the moment that he was a single person – has followed the traditional scheme; but in general he likes to approach the subject afresh, and this accords well with the realistic and experimental nature of the sculpture.

COMPOSITIONS (fig. 18 and pp. 182-4). Scale dictated the approximate size of the figures in the metopes, and this meant that only two, or at most three, could be fitted into each. The number of ways in which two, or three, figures can be arranged within an almost square field is limited, and sophisticated artists have been at pains to disguise the simplicity of such compositions by obscuring the divisions between the main elements of the design. The designer of the Olympian metopes disdained such devices, and was not ashamed to reveal and even to stress the simple geometrical schemes on which his designs were based. He thought, and thought rightly, that in this way they harmonized better with the powerful architectural members which enframed them. So we have the design of the three verticals, of the cross, of the triangle, and of others readily apparent. All this is in keeping with the general spirit of the building, its solid honesty and its freedom from pretence.

NATURE OF THE LEGENDS. There was another element which the designer found ready to his hand, well attuned to his own temper, and that was the simple logic and earthy humour of the folk-tales in which the Labours of Herakles were recorded. The hero is set a seemingly impossible task: it is a trick or puzzle, sometimes little more than a verbal puzzle, and he solves it in the folk-tales by another trick. For instance the trick with the Nemean lion was that it was invulnerable, it could not be wounded. Herakles solved this by knocking it senseless with his club and then strangling it. The stables of Augeias had to be cleansed in one day. Herakles' solution was the water of the Alpheios.

CHARACTER OF HERAKLES AND HIS HELPERS. But although he keeps to the story, the designer likes to think out each problem for himself, to put himself in the place of his hero, to re-create his feelings and the emotional content of the situation, and to face and overcome in a commonsense way the practical difficulties. Accordingly, his Herakles, who passes from youth to age before our eyes, is single-minded like himself, intent only on the task in hand. He is strong, but not immeasurably so, and is without a trace of the boasting, the stupidity, and the raw self-indulgence which often degrade the Herakles of later literature and art. Further, the tale is lifted above the level of folk-lore by the parts which Athena and Hermes play in it, parts hinted but not elaborated by archaic artists. On each of the four occasions when Athena is present she shows a different and sympathetic aspect of her traditional character. She gives robust encouragement or sound technical advice, accords gracious recognition or displays divine power. Hermes serves as friend and guide at the beginning, and reappears when his special knowledge of the difficult way to the Underworld is essential. These quasi-historical touches deepen the interest, enrich the content, and enhance the credibility of the legend.

ARRANGEMENT. It is clear from the account of Pausanias how the metopes were arranged when he saw them. By mistake he mentions only eleven, omitting that with Kerberos, but if we insert this at the east end of the temple last but one to the north, the find-spots of the fragments confirm the order he gives. This is, at the west end, the girdle of the Amazon queen, the Keryneian hind, the Cretan bull, the Stymphalian birds, the Hydra, the Nemean lion; and on the east, the Erymanthian boar, the mares of Diomedes the Thracian, the fight with Geryon, the apples of the Hesperides, Kerberos, the Augeian stables.

The twelve labours fall naturally into two groups of six each, one group comprising the labours performed on home ground, in or near the Peloponnese; the other those performed abroad, sometimes at the ends of the earth. The two groups of six over the east and west porticos at Olympia did not, when recorded by Pausanias, correspond with these two; but it has been suggested that originally they did, and that the order was changed during one of the major restorations of the building, probably that when the pedimental figures were restored and adjusted. By moving the metopes of the bull and the Amazon round on to the east and substituting for them those of the boar and the stables, the two groups could be made to correspond. It has further been suggested that within these groups also the metopes should be rearranged, the main argument being that each metope was designed to be seen from a certain point of view and that its composition tells best only from that position (See *Bibliography* p. 187, no. 5.). The rearrangement suggested is:

West Side: (North) Birds, Boar, Lion, Hydra, Hind, Stables (South)

East Side: (South) Horses, Amazon, Apples, Geryon, Kerberos, Bull (North)

These arguments are based on much careful observation and acute reasoning, and some at least of the conclusions may well be correct, but for our purpose it is better to study the two groups as they certainly were in the time of Pausanias, though on the west we will do so in reverse order, because in this way we can start with the labour traditionally regarded as the first: the killing of the Nemean lion, or, as Pausanias calls it, the lion in the land of Argos.

THE LION OF NEMEA. Archaic artists delighted to depict the struggle itself, and despite the 143–151 literary tradition of the preliminary clubbing, the lion is usually far from insensible. At Olympia the fight is over: the monster lies dead, and the hero, with one foot on its body, rests his head on his hand in a state of exhaustion. His brow is wrinkled not in exhaustion only, but at the prospect of the years of toil ahead. He is not alone, but is accompanied by two other children of Zeus, Athena and Hermes. He takes no notice of them, and we are left in doubt whether he sees them or not, but their presence at the outset is significant: it reminds us of the promise that when the labours had been performed Herakles should be granted immortality, and that, until then, he has divine help. Athena is austere but kindly; with the firm kindness that offers not comfort but moral support for fresh effort. The plump lion, its limbs carefully disposed, has a faintly comic air. Its head and body are perhaps a replacement made when the temple had been damaged a generation or two after its erection, and carved by a conscientious sculptor trying to imitate the style of the original sculptor but failing to capture its spirit. The usual version of the myth makes Herakles flay the lion and afterwards carry its skin about with him. This skin, and his club, as we see from Athenian vase-pictures, had already become his conventional tokens. They are often an encumbrance to the artist: at Olympia the lion's skin is ignored, and the club introduced only when it is useful.

THE HYDRA OF LERNA. The second metope is the Hydra of Lerna, a monstrous many- 152 headed water-snake which, when one of its heads was cut off, grew another or several others in its place. In vase-pictures Herakles was often accompanied by his faithful nephew Iolaos, who deals with the great crab, ally of the Hydra. Here there is no crab and no nephew, but Herakles treats the Hydra in the traditional way, burning the stumps of the severed necks in order to prevent revival.

THE BIRDS OF STYMPHALOS. The next metope, that of the Stymphalian birds, is one of the 153–161 most unexpected and most charming creations of ancient art. Again the action is over, and Herakles, now bearded, has come to thank his patroness and to show his spoils. Athena is goddess of the rock, not only of the Acropolis rock at Athens but of citadels everywhere. The rock on which she is seated, and her heavy aegis, symbolize her eternal task as the guardian and the warrior. A gracious youthful figure, she looks approvingly down at the gift which

Herakles has brought her, the proof of his success in exterminating the dangerous birds of the Stymphalian marshes.

162-168   THE CRETAN BULL. The enormous Cretan bull was of doubtful pedigree: some said that it was the bull of whom Pasiphae was enamoured and thus the sire of the Minotaur: others that it was the bull that carried Europa to Crete; but that was generally considered to have been Zeus himself. Whatever its origin, Herakles was given the task of capturing it, and he is seen fully engaged: he has managed to rope the animal and is throwing all his weight backwards to turn it and so bring it under control.

From both the artistic and the technical point of view this was an awkward subject. The almost square metope-panel can with difficulty accommodate a lengthy animal whose scale must agree roughly with that of the human figure which is already fixed. The human body must overlap the animal, and this demands great depth of modelling unless the animal is to appear insubstantial: depth of modelling implies a high projection of the figures from the background, no easy matter with marble, which has great weight and low tensile strength.

The means by which these difficulties have been overcome will be clear if the metope is studied for a while, but a few of them may be mentioned. The animal is set diagonally and not horizontally in the square, and its head is turned back: these two devices, one of which extends the space it can occupy whilst the other reduces its own length, allows its size to be greatly increased, an important point when its size was the main point of the story. The turning of the head forced the designer to foreshorten the neck – and it is an interesting early example of foreshortening in sculpture – but it made the design more compact, neatly framed the bull's head against its own body, and heightened the emotional tension by bringing the man and the beast face to face. The problem of the high projection of the marble is solved by recessing the central part of the bull's body so that the powerful torso of Herakles, almost in the round and set off admirably against the animal's broad, flat contours, can rest within it. The carving of his head is bold and almost harsh, matching the rugged torso. It is a pity that so many of the limbs are missing: with the bull's tail and the hero's club they formed a complex and satisfying pattern fringing the main chiastic design. Enough colour remained on this metope when it was found to show that the bull was red and the background blue.

169-172   THE KERYNEIAN HIND. The Keryneian hind belonged to Artemis, and was not to be killed, but taken alive. There is no emotional interest in this, the least exciting of the Labours, and accordingly, as in the metope of the bull, the designer naturally concentrates on its physical aspect. Only a few fragments remain: but it is clear that the compact design was basically triangular, with Herakles kneeling on the animal's back.

169 171,   THE GIRDLE OF THE AMAZON. In the Labour of the Amazon's girdle the head of the Amazon
173, 175   queen herself, who is dead or dying, is an interesting study, but for realism equalled or even

surpassed by the head of a dying man in the west pediment of the temple at Aegina, carved fifteen or twenty years before (Richter, *Archaic Greek Art*, fig. 251). This is the more savage version of the legend: Herakles does not merely tear off the magic girdle of the Amazon, but kills her before doing so. For the changes lately made in the reconstruction of this metope see p. 182.

We now move round to the eastern side of the building, describing the metopes in the order given by Pausanias, and starting on the south.

THE ERYMANTHIAN BOAR. The Labour of the Erymanthian boar had a long artistic tradi- 174, 176
tion, and it can be seen from the remains of this metope, again very fragmentary, that the designer had been content to copy in essentials the ordinary scheme used by vase-painters. When Herakles had captured the boar and was bringing it back to the palace of Eurystheus at Tiryns, the king, knowing that he was on his way, took refuge in one of the huge storage-jars that were used for keeping grain and other comestibles in Mycenean and later palaces. Herakles is usually shown dumping the boar on top of him, and one of the sandstone metopes of the treasury at the mouth of the Silaris near Paestum has an amusing refinement on this: it shows Eurystheus well inside the jar and pulling down over himself, apparently just in time, its hinged bronze lid. At Olympia the ordinary design is followed, but there is not room for the whole jar: the shape looks abnormal, but this is because part of it was to be thought of as out of sight.

THE MARES OF DIOMEDES. Of the man-eating mares of King Diomedes of Thrace, which 177-179
became tame after Herakles had fed them with the flesh of their master, only one was shown, and of that only a fragment of the head survives. The composition was again that of the body of Herakles crossing that of the animal, but so far as one can judge was less dynamic than in the metope of the Cretan bull.

GERYON. Geryon was a three-bodied giant who lived in the extreme west of the world, and 180-185
owned great herds of cattle attended by a herdsman and a dog: the legend is precise, and both their names are known. Herakles killed dependants and master in succession, and brought the cattle back. Vase-painters are able to show the whole proceeding, but the designer of the metope has wisely omitted everything except the fight with Geryon himself, a subject difficult enough because of the necessarily unconvincing anatomy of the monster, who is fully armed with three panoplies, including shields. From what remains it is not possible to restore the exact composition, but two of Geryon's bodies seem to be defunct: one head is trailing, the eyes glazing and the mouth hanging open. Herakles treads down the tangled mass, and raises his club in a desperate attempt to dispatch the remaining third: something of his desperation can be seen by the sculptor's various touches in brows and eyes, lips, and nostrils.

186-193   THE APPLES OF THE HESPERIDES. The golden apples of the Tree of Life must, at least in
one of the versions of the legend, have been the last of the Labours, since the apples were the
symbols of the immortality which Herakles had been promised when the full number of his
tasks was completed. The tree which bore them grew in the gardens of the Hesperides. These
lay in the north of Africa: the giant Atlas who is associated with the story must be a personifi-
cation of the mountains to which the name is still attached. In one version of the legend,
especially popular at the end of the fifth century in Athens, Herakles goes to the gardens himself
and obtains the apples through the connivance of the guardian nymphs; but in another, which
is that followed here, he persuades the giant Atlas to fetch them for him, offering to bear
meanwhile his vast burden of the heavens. The Atlas range was the greatest and wildest near
the shores of the Mediterranean, and the idea that the sky was supported on its shoulders would
have arisen quite naturally.

Pausanias may have misunderstood the action here, for he speaks of Herakles being about to
receive the burden (*forema*) of Atlas, and stilted though the style of Pausanias is, this word
could hardly be applied to the apples which Atlas is holding in his hands, whilst it is Herakles
who supports the sky. Herakles has a cushion, partly to ease the burden, partly to give him
extra height, for like many strong men he was, as Pindar tells us, not particularly tall; and
Atlas was a giant. These matter-of-fact details, which might easily have been humorous, are
introduced in such a straightforward and sensible way that they seem natural. In several versions
of the story this was an awkward moment: Atlas refused to resume his burden and Herakles
had no prospect of freeing himself. At Olympia nothing so unseemly occurs. Athena is in
control; for the designer, always sensitive to practical and personal difficulties, and to the
consistency and credibility of the legend, sees that her intervention is essential. She is daughter
of Zeus, god of the sky, and therefore capable of supporting, even with one hand, the whole
weight of the heavens for a moment, so that the interchange can take place. Although there is
so little action, the whole scene – with patient hero, impassive giant, and the deity intervening,
as often in Greek tragedy, to resolve a crisis – is charged with dramatic force and a sense of
impending release and fulfilment.

194-201   KERBEROS. Pausanias does not mention this metope, but it must have come between that of
the Hesperides and the last of the series on the north. The capture of Kerberos seems a somewhat
pointless exercise, since it consisted simply in dragging up into the daylight the dog who
guarded the gate of Hades, showing him to Eurystheus, and then returning him to his post.
Yet it is the only one of the Labours mentioned in Homer, and it takes on a different and a fuller
meaning if it is recognized as the relic of an older and more elaborate legend in which Herakles
overcame not only the guardian of the gate but Hades himself, and so attained his immortality.

Only the head, shoulders, and forelegs of Kerberos appear in the lower right corner of the
metope: the rest is hidden in the mouth of hell, and in this way the designer has given himself
much more room for manoeuvre. Hermes, rather than Athena, was present, and the reason

is clear: Hermes is the divine psychagogos, who leads the souls of the dead into the Underworld, and it is he who knows the dark and difficult way to its entrance. Herakles had a chain round the animal's neck and is trying to dislodge him. This contest differs from that with the Cretan bull, for it is one not of strength against strength but of strength and skill against strength and cunning. The temper of the animal must be gauged, and the right moment chosen for relaxing or increasing the strain: there is always a danger that the hell-hound, instead of obstinately resisting, may suddenly decide to attack, and rid himself once for all of his tormentor. The niceties of this situation can be read in the poise of Herakles' head, his wary eyes, and the nervous lines of nostrils and lips. His torso is fully modelled as if he were naked, but the folds of drapery round the hips show that in fact he was wearing a thin garment, perhaps as a shield against the heat, so thin that it was carved only at its lower edge, the rest being simply a coat of paint.

194-197

200

THE AUGEIAN STABLES. The last metope Pausanias mentions is that of the oxen of Augeias. Augeias was king of Elis, and his vast herds threatened to overwhelm the whole land with their dung. Herakles offered to clean the stables in one day, the reward to be so many head of cattle. The king, thinking he had nothing to lose, entered into the bargain. Herakles breached the wall of the stables in two places: through one of them he let in the waters of the Alpheios and the Peneios: through the other he let them out again with their surge of filth. Herakles has a crowbar in his hands, and, with an expression of anger and disgust, is breaking down the wall under the instructions of Athena, who points to the appropriate place with her spear: this was made separately of bronze. She also wears a helmet which had cheek-pieces, and has a shield beside her; it is seen edgeways and disappears into the background: this is a kind of silhouette-contour analogous to the silhouette-formulae common on sixth-century vases, where the painter reproduces the exact frontal aspect of a complicated object, not attempting to foreshorten, but merely omitting, what lies behind. A small naturalistic detail may be noted, the fold of skin between thumb and forefinger as they rest on the rim of the shield: this is a characteristic piece of observation and the same area has been the subject of special study in the hand of the youth (Q) in the west pediment. Athena's dress is the Doric peplos, not the simplest form but that girded under the overfall, as worn by Hippodameia (K) in the east pediment. The head of this Athena is the least sensitive and least interesting of the four in the metopes, possibly because it was half-hidden by the cheek-pieces of the helmet; and the body, though monumental in its main design, is summary in execution. Set exactly frontal, however, it provides a powerful vertical mass on the right of the metope, to which the cross-latticed pattern of the rest of the composition is anchored.

202-211

83

19

Because it was performed in the heart of their country this exploit of Herakles had a special interest for the inhabitants of Elis: but it had an even greater importance for the Greek world as a whole, because its completion was the prelude to his marking out of the Sacred Precinct, and his institution of the Olympic Festival.

THE CULT-STATUE

At an unknown date, but probably several years after the temple was built, the Athenian sculptor Pheidias was commissioned to make for it a cult-image of Zeus on a colossal scale. This was to be a seated figure about forty feet high, in a technique of gold and ivory which the Greeks seem to have learnt originally from the East. The main framework of the figure must have been of wood, and to this were fixed plates of gold for the drapery. The flesh was composed of sheets of ivory pieced together, and since no elephant-tusk is more than about six inches in diameter, the number of these pieces must have been very great. The elaborate throne on which the figure sat was also plated with gold, inlaid with ebony, semi-precious stones and glass, and was adorned with paintings, reliefs, and statuettes. Pausanias has left us a detailed description of the statue and its throne, and bronze coins of Hadrian between A.D. 133 and 137 reproduce a statue of Zeus seated, and also a head of Zeus, both of which may be miniature copies of it (figs. 12, 13); but naturally they tell us little about its style. Of the statue itself nothing now remains, and the date and manner of its destruction are unknown: some think that it perished in the temple in the fifth century A.D., but others accept the story told by a Byzantine author that it was carried off to Constantinople and set up in a palace which was burnt down, also in the fifth century A.D.

Just outside the precinct at Olympia to the south are the remains of a building known in antiquity as the workshop of Pheidias, in which, Pausanias says, the statue was manufactured piece by piece. German excavations of 1954–58 revealed, under the floor of this building, debris of a kind which one might expect to find if a colossal statue in this technique had been made there – chips of ivory, cores of elephant-tusks, one or two metal-workers' tools, pieces of glass prepared for inlay; and a series of terracotta moulds, apparently used for shaping the golden drapery of the statue, although the method of doing so is not clear.

Among this debris were found fragments of Athenian pottery of a style which can be dated round 435 B.C. This suggests that Pheidias completed the statue of Zeus in the period between the dedication, in 438 B.C., of his other colossal gold-and-ivory statue, that of Athena Parthenos in the Parthenon at Athens, and his death in 432 B.C. The commission for the Zeus could, however, have been given to him before the Athena Parthenos was finished, and drawings, models, estimates, and arrangements for the supply of material could have been made before the main work of constructing it was finally undertaken. In any case, it looks as if the temple stood for twenty years before the statue by Pheidias occupied it. There may have been an earlier statue in the interval, but if so its memory was obscured by the fame of the Pheidian statue, to the majesty of which many ancient writers testify. (Bibliography, p. 188.)

ἐποιήθη δὲ ὁ ναὸς καὶ τὸ ἄγαλμα τῷ Διὶ ἀπὸ λαφύ-
ρων, ἡνίκα Πίσαν οἱ Ἠλεῖοι καὶ ὅσον τῶν περιοίκων
ἄλλο συναπέστη Πισαίοις πολέμῳ καθεῖλον. Φειδίαν
δὲ τὸν ἐργασάμενον τὸ ἄγαλμα εἶναι καὶ ἐπίγραμμά
ἐστιν ἐς μαρτυρίαν ὑπὸ τοῦ Διὸς γεγραμμένον τοῖς
ποσί·

   Φειδίας Χαρμίδου υἱὸς Ἀθηναῖός μ' ἐποίησε.

τοῦ ναοῦ δὲ Δώριος μέν ἐστιν ἡ ἐργασία, τὰ δὲ ἐκτὸς
περίστυλός ἐστι· πεποίηται δὲ ἐπιχωρίου πώρου. ὕψος
μὲν δὴ αὐτοῦ ⟨τὸ⟩ ἐς τὸν ἀετὸν ἀνῆκον, εἰσὶν οἱ ὀκτὼ
πόδες καὶ ἑξήκοντα, εὖρος δὲ πέντε καὶ ἐνενήκοντα,
τὰ δὲ ἐς μῆκος τριάκοντά τε καὶ διακόσιοι· τέκτων δὲ
ἐγένετο αὐτοῦ Λίβων ἐπιχώριος. . . .
ἐν δὲ Ὀλυμπίᾳ λέβης ἐπίχρυσος ἐπὶ ἑκάστῳ τοῦ
ὀρόφου τῷ πέρατι ἐπίκειται καὶ Νίκη κατὰ μέσον
μάλιστα ἕστηκε τὸν ἀετόν, ἐπίχρυσος καὶ αὕτη. ὑπὸ
δὲ τῆς Νίκης τὸ ἄγαλμα ἀσπὶς ἀνάκειται χρυσῆ, Μέ-
δουσαν τὴν Γοργόνα ἔχουσα ἐπειργασμένην. τὸ ἐπί-
γραμμα δὲ τὸ ἐπὶ τῇ ἀσπίδι τούς τε ἀναθέντας δηλοῖ
καὶ καθ' ἥντινα αἰτίαν ἀνέθεσαν· λέγει γὰρ δὴ οὕτω·

  ναὸς μὲν φιάλαν χρυσέαν ἔχει, ἐκ δὲ Τανάγρας
    τοὶ Λακεδαιμόνιοι συμμαχία τ' ἀν⟨έ⟩θεν
  δῶρον ἀπ' Ἀργείων καὶ Ἀθαναίων καὶ Ἰώνων,
    τὰν δεκάταν νίκας εἵνεκα τῶ πολέμω. . . .

τὰ δὲ ἐν τοῖς ἀετοῖς, ἔστιν ἔμπροσθεν Πέλοπος ἡ
πρὸς Οἰνόμαον τῶν ἵππων ἅμιλλα ἔτι μέλλουσα καὶ
τὸ ἔργον τοῦ δρόμου παρὰ ἀμφοτέρων ἐν παρασκευῇ.
Διὸς δὲ ἀγάλματος κατὰ μέσον πεποιημένου μάλιστα
τὸν ἀετόν, ἔστιν Οἰνόμαος ἐν δεξιᾷ τοῦ Διὸς ἐπι-
κείμενος κράνος τῇ κεφαλῇ, παρὰ δὲ αὐτὸν γυνὴ
Στερόπη, θυγατέρων καὶ αὕτη τῶν Ἄτλαντος· Μυρτί-
λος δέ, ὃς ἤλαυνε τῷ Οἰνομάῳ τὸ ἅρμα, κάθηται
πρὸ τῶν ἵππων, οἱ δέ εἰσιν ἀριθμὸν οἱ ἵπποι τέσσαρες.
μετὰ δὲ αὐτόν εἰσιν ἄνδρες δύο· ὀνόματα μέν σφισιν
οὐκ ἔστι, θεραπεύειν δὲ ἄρα τοὺς ἵππους καὶ τούτοις
προσετέτακτο ὑπὸ τοῦ Οἰνομάου. πρὸς αὐτῷ δὲ
κατάκειται τῷ πέρατι Κλάδεος· ἔχει δὲ καὶ ἐς τὰ
ἄλλα παρ' Ἠλείων τιμὰς ποταμῶν μάλιστα μετά γε
Ἀλφειόν. τὰ δὲ ἐς ἀριστερὰ ἀπὸ τοῦ Διὸς ὁ Πέλοψ
καὶ Ἱπποδάμεια καὶ ὅ τε ἡνίοχός ἐστι τοῦ Πέλοπος
καὶ ἵπποι δύο τε ἄνδρες, ἱπποκόμοι δὴ καὶ οὗτοι τῷ
Πέλοπι. καὶ αὖθις ὁ ἀετὸς κάτεισιν ἐς στενόν, καὶ
κατὰ τοῦτο Ἀλφειὸς ἐπ' αὐτοῦ πεποίηται. τῷ δὲ
ἀνδρὶ ὃς ἡνιοχεῖ τῷ Πέλοπι λόγῳ μὲν τῷ Τροιζηνίων
ἐστὶν ὄνομα Σφαῖρος, ὁ δὲ ἐξηγητὴς ἔφασκεν ὁ ἐν
Ὀλυμπίᾳ Κίλλαν εἶναι. τὰ μὲν δὴ ἔμπροσθεν ⟨ἐν⟩

2. The temple and the statue were made for Zeus from
spoils when the Eleans destroyed in war Pisa and those
of the surrounding inhabitants who conspired with the
Pisatans. That the statue was made by Pheidias is shown
by the inscription below at the feet of Zeus:

'Pheidias, son of Charmides, an Athenian, made me'.

The temple is of Doric work, and there is a colonnade
round it.

3. It is built of local limestone. Its height up to the
gable is sixty-eight feet, its breadth ninety-five, its
length two hundred and thirty: its builder was Libon,
a native. . . .

4. In Olympia a gilded cauldron stands on each corner
of the roof, and a Victory, also gilded, on the pediment,
in the middle. Under the statue of Victory is set a golden
shield having the head of the Gorgon Medusa wrought
on it. The inscription on the shield explains who the
dedicators were and why they dedicated it. It runs
thus:

  'The temple has a golden shield: from Tanagra
    the Spartans and their alliance dedicated it,
  as a gift, from Argives, Athenians, and Ionians,
    the tenth part from victory in the war.' . . .

6. As for what is in the pediments, in front there is the
contest with horses between Pelops and Oinomaos
about to begin, and preparation for the race is being
made by both. There is a statue of Zeus right in the
middle of the pediment: Oinomaos is on the right of
Zeus, with a helmet on his head, and by him his wife
Sterope, one of the daughters of Atlas. Myrtilos too,
who drove the chariot of Oinomaos, sits in front of the
horses: the horses are four in number. After him are
two men: they have no names, but they too must have
been ordered by Oinomaos to look after the horses.
Right in the corner lies Kladeos: after Alpheios he is
the most honoured by the Eleans of all rivers. On the
left from Zeus is Pelops, and Hippodameia, and the
charioteer of Pelops, and horses, and two men, and they
also are grooms for Pelops. And again the pediment
narrows down, and here Alpheios is represented in it.
According to the Troizenians the name of the man
who drove for Pelops is Sphairos, but the guide at
Olympia said it was Killas.

Of the sculptures in the pediments those in front are by

τοῖς ἀετοῖς ἐστι Παιωνίου, γένος ἐκ Μένδης τῆς
Θρᾳκίας, τὰ δὲ ὄπισθεν αὐτῶν Ἀλκαμένους, ἀνδρὸς
ἡλικίαν τε κατὰ Φειδίαν καὶ δευτερεῖα ἐνεγκαμένου
σοφίας ἐς ποίησιν ἀγαλμάτων. τὰ δὲ ἐν τοῖς ἀετοῖς
ἐστιν αὐτῷ Λαπιθῶν ἐν τῷ Πειρίθου γάμῳ πρὸς Κεν-
ταύρους ἡ μάχη. κατὰ μὲν δὴ τοῦ ἀετοῦ τὸ μέσον
Πειρίθους ἐστίν· παρὰ δὲ αὐτὸν τῇ μὲν Εὐρυτίων
ἡρπακὼς τὴν γυναῖκά ἐστι τοῦ Πειρίθου καὶ ἀμύνων
Καινεὺς τῷ Πειρίθῳ, τῇ δὲ Θησεὺς ἀμυνόμενος
πελέκει τοὺς Κενταύρους· Κένταυρος δὲ ὁ μὲν παρ-
θένον, ὁ δὲ παῖδα ἡρπακώς ἐστιν ὡραῖον. ἐποίησε δὲ
ἐμοὶ δοκεῖν ταῦτα ὁ Ἀλκαμένης, Πειρίθουν τε εἶναι
Διὸς ἐν ἔπεσι τοῖς Ὁμήρου δεδιδαγμένος καὶ Θησέα
ἐπιστάμενος ὡς εἴη τέταρτος ἀπὸ Πέλοπος.

ἔστι δὲ ἐν Ὀλυμπίᾳ καὶ Ἡρακλέους τὰ πολλὰ τῶν
ἔργων. ὑπὲρ μὲν τοῦ ναοῦ πεποίηται τῶν θυρῶν ἡ
ἐξ Ἀρκαδίας ἄργα τοῦ ὑὸς καὶ τὰ πρὸς Διομήδην
τὸν Θρᾷκα καὶ ἐν Ἐρυθείᾳ πρὸς Γηρυόνην, καὶ
Ἄτλαντός τε τὸ φόρημα ἐκδέχεσθαι μέλλων καὶ τῆς
κόπρου καθαίρων τὴν γῆν ἐστιν Ἠλείοις· ὑπὲρ δὲ τοῦ
ὀπισθοδόμου τῶν θυρῶν τοῦ ζωστῆρος τὴν Ἀμαζόνα
ἐστὶν ἀφαιρούμενος καὶ τὰ ἐς τὴν ἔλαφον καὶ τὸν ἐν
Κνωσσῷ ταῦρον καὶ ὄρνιθας τὰς ἐπὶ Στυμφήλῳ καὶ
ἐς ὕδραν τε καὶ τὸν ἐν τῇ γῇ τῇ Ἀργείᾳ λέοντα.

Paionios, of Mende in Thrace by birth, those at the
back by Alkamenes, a man of the same age as Pheidias
and adjudged second to him in skill in the making of
statues. His work in the pediments is the fight of Lapiths
against Centaurs at the wedding of Peirithoos. In the
middle of the pediment is Peirithoos: beside him on the
one side is Eurytion who has seized the wife of Peirithoos, and Kaineus defending Peirithoos; on the other
side Theseus defending himself against the centaurs
with an axe: one centaur has seized a girl, the other a
beautiful boy. Alkamenes I think created this because
he had learnt from Homer's poems that Peirithoos was
the son of Zeus, and knowing that Theseus was a
great-grandson of Pelops.

9. Most of the labours of Herakles are in Olympia.
Above the doors of the temple is represented the hunt-
ing of the boar from Arkadia, and the exploit against
Diomedes the Thracian, and in Erytheia against Geryon,
and Herakles about to receive the burden of Atlas, and
cleansing the land of dung for the Eleans. Above the
doors of the room at the back is Herakles taking the
girdle of the Amazon, and the affair with the hind, and
the bull in Knossos, and the birds on Stymphalos, and
the hydra and the lion in the land of Argos.

PLATES

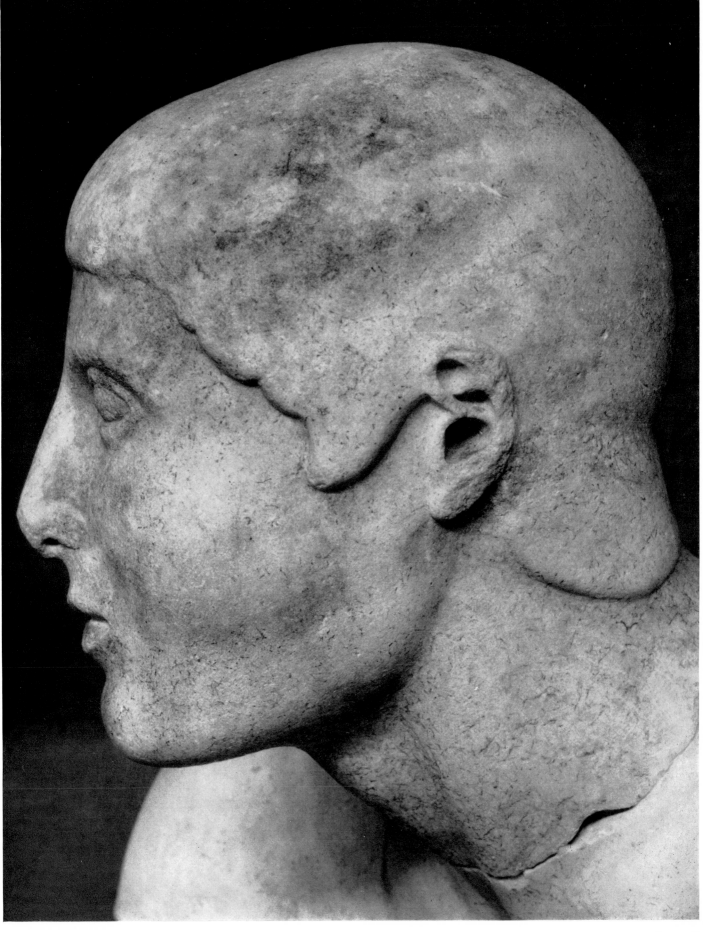

1. River-god (Kladeos or Alpheios)

2. River-god (Alpheios or Kladeos)   East pediment A

3. River-god (Alpheios or Kladeos)   East pediment A

4. River-god (Kladeos or Alpheios)   East pediment P

5. River-god (Kladeos or Alpheios)   East pediment P

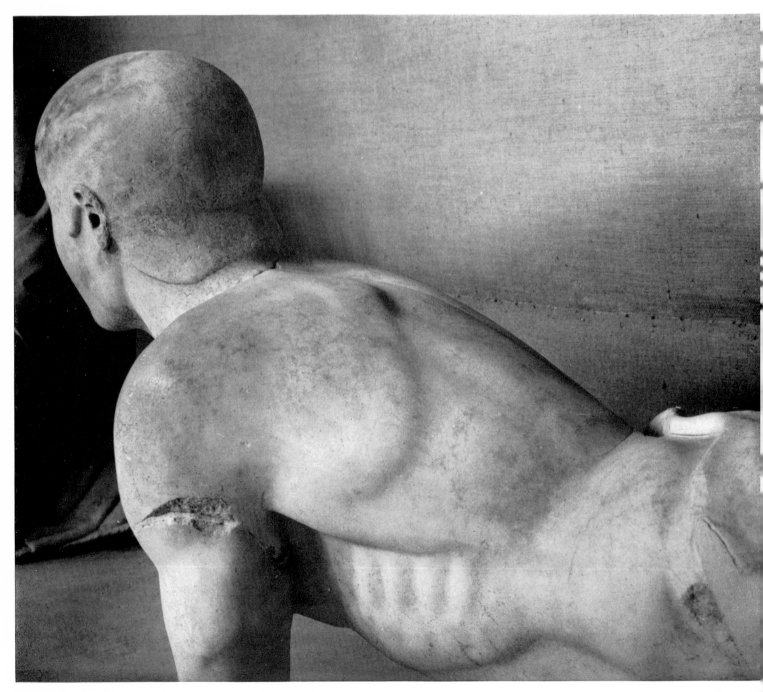

6. River-god (Kladeos or Alpheios)

7. River-god (Kladeos or Alpheios)

East pediment P

8. River-god (Kladeos or Alpheios)   East pediment P   9. River-god (Kladeos or Alpheios)   East pediment P

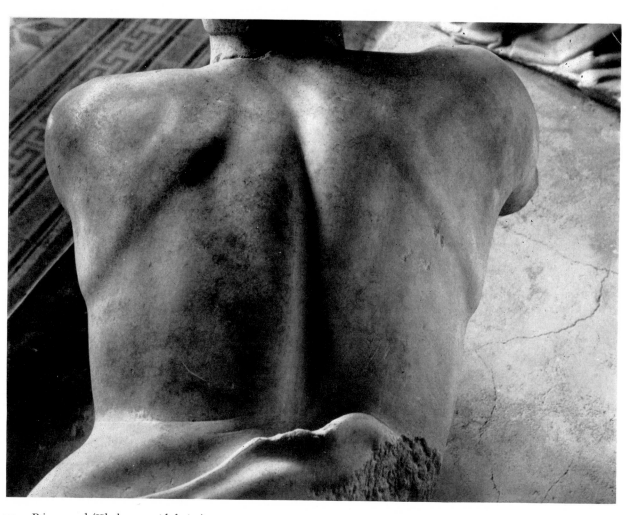

10. River-god (Kladeos or Alpheios)   East pediment P

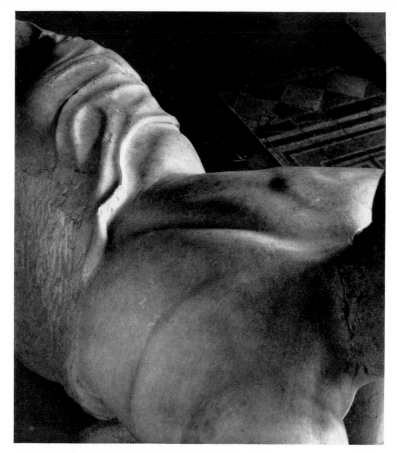

11. River-god (Kladeos or Alpheios)   East pediment P

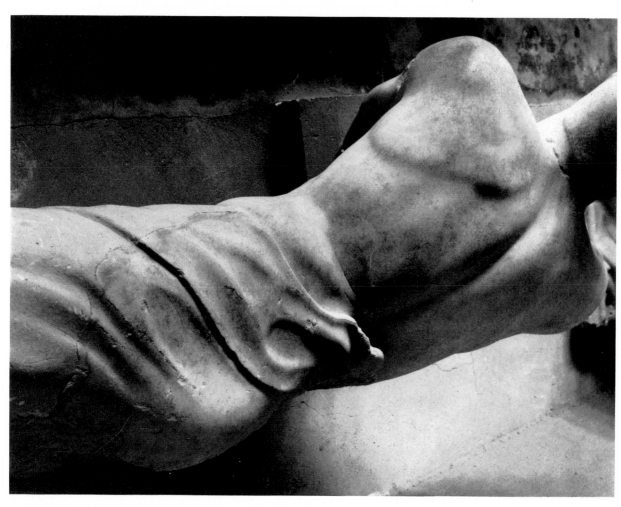

12. River-god (Kladeos or Alpheios)   East pediment P

13. Zeus

East pediment H

14.   Zeus   East pediment H

15. Oinomaos   East pediment I

16. Hippodameia (or Sterope)   East pediment K   17. Hippodameia (or Sterope)   East pediment K

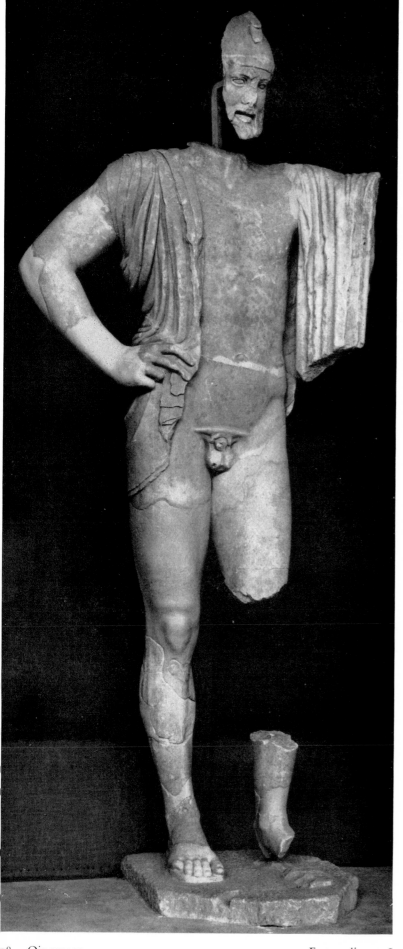

18. Oinomaos   East pediment I   19. Hippodameia (or Sterope)   East pediment K

20. Oinomaos

East pediment I

21. Hippodameia (or Sterope) East pediment K

22. Kneeling girl

East pediment O

23.   Kneeling girl   East pediment O

24. Kneeling girl

25. Kneeling girl   East pediment O

26. Kneeling girl   East pediment O   27. Kneeling girl   East pediment O

28. Chariot horses of Oinomaos (or Pelops)　　　　　　　　East pediment M

29. Chariot horse of Oinomaos (or Pelops)　　　　　　　　East pediment M

Chariot horses of Oinomaos (or Pelops)   East pediment M

31. Seer, perhaps Iamos

32. Seer, perhaps Iamos

33. Seer, perhaps Iamos

34. Seer, perhaps Iamos

35. Seer, perhaps Iamos

36. Seer, perhaps Iamos

37. Seer, perhaps Iamos   East pediment N

38. Seer, perhaps Iamos   East pediment N

39. Seer, perhaps Iamos   East pediment N

40. Seer, perhaps Iamos   East pediment N

41. Seated boy, perhaps Arkas

East pediment E

42.   Seated boy, perhaps Arkas   East pediment E

43. Seated boy, perhaps Arkas

East pediment E

44. Sterope (or Hippodameia)   East pediment F

45. Sterope (or Hippodameia)   East pediment F

46. Pelops   East pediment G

47. Pelops   East pediment G

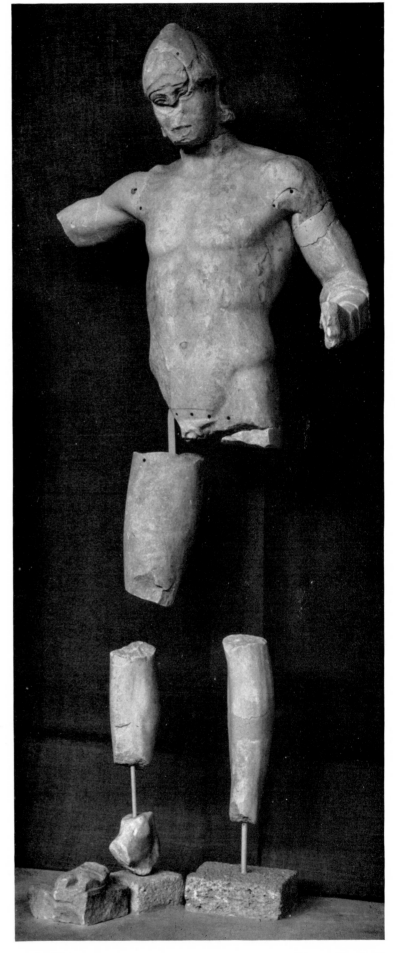

48. Sterope (or Hippodameia)   East pediment F   49. Pelops   East pediment G

50. Kneeling youth (Myrtilos?)   East pediment B

51. Kneeling youth (Myrtilos?)   East pediment B

52. Kneeling youth (Myrtilos?)   East pediment B

53. Chariot horses of Pelops (or Oinomaos) East pediment D

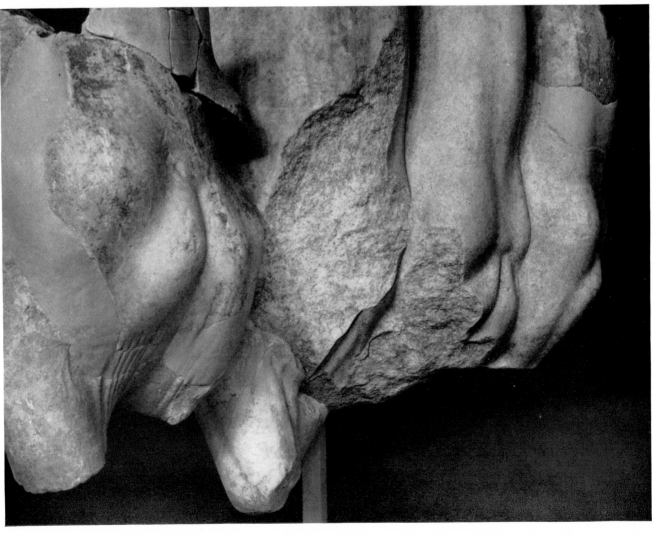

54. Chariot horses of Pelops (or Oinomaos) East pediment D

55. Charioteer

56. Charioteer

57. Charioteer

East pediment C

58. Seer   East pediment L

59.   Seer   East pediment L

60.   Seer   East pediment L   61.   Seer   East pediment L

62. Lapith woman

West pediment A

63. Lapith woman

West pediment A

64. Old Lapith woman

West pediment B

65. Old Lapith woman

West pediment V

66. Lapith woman

West pediment U

67. Old Lapith woman   West pediment B

68.　Old Lapith woman

69. Old Lapith woman

West pediment B

70. Lapith woman

West pediment V

71. Lapith youth

72.　Lapith youth

73. Lapith youth, Centaur and Lapith girl

74. Centaur   West pediment D

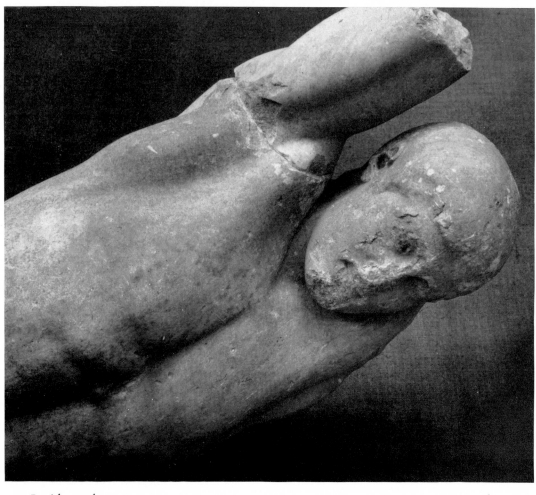

75. Lapith youth   West pediment C

76.   Centaur

77. Centaur

78. Lapith girl

79. Lapith girl

West pediment E

80. Lapith girl

West pediment E

81. Lapith girl

82. Centaur   West pediment P

83. Lapith youth   West pediment Q

84. Centaur   West pediment P

85. Lapith youth   West pediment Q

86. Centaur and Lapith youth

87. Centaur and Lapith youth

West pediment P, Q

88. Lapith youth

West pediment Q

89.   Centaur

90. Lapith youth

West pediment Q

91. Lapith youth

West pediment Q

92. Theseus and Centaur

93. Theseus   West pediment M

94. Theseus   West pediment M

95. Theseus

96. Theseus

97. Theseus

98.   Centaur and Lapith woman

99. Centaur

100. Lapith woman, companion of the bride West pediment O

101. Apollo

West pediment L

102.   Apollo   West pediment L

103.   Apollo   West pediment L   104.   Apollo   West pediment L

105. Apollo

106. Apollo

107. Apollo

108. Apollo

109. Apollo

110. Deidameia and the centaur Eurytion   West pediment H, I

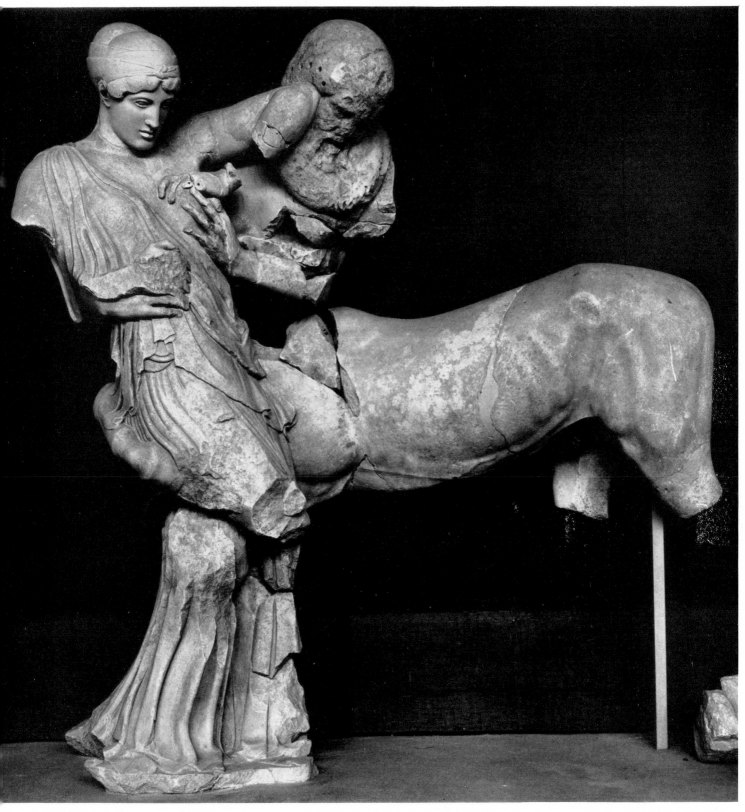

11. Deidameia and the centaur Eurytion

112. Deidameia

113. Deidameia

114. Deidameia

115. The centaur Eurytion

116. Deidameia and the centaur Eurytion   West pediment H, I

118. Peirithoos   West pediment K   119. Peirithoos   West pediment K

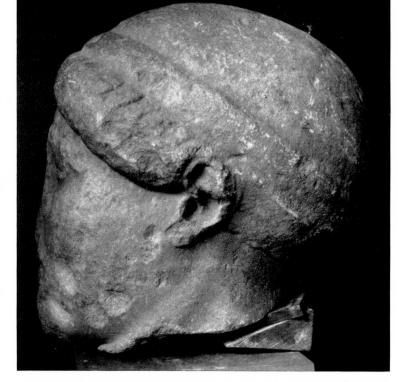

120. Peirithoos   West pediment K   121. Peirithoos   West pediment K

122. Centaur   West pediment G   123. Centaur   West pediment G

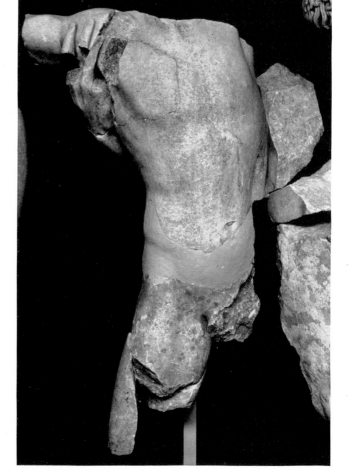

124. Lapith boy   West pediment F   125. Lapith boy   West pediment F

126. Lapith boy and centaur

West pediment F, G

127. Lapith girl, centaur and Lapith youth

West pediment R, S, T

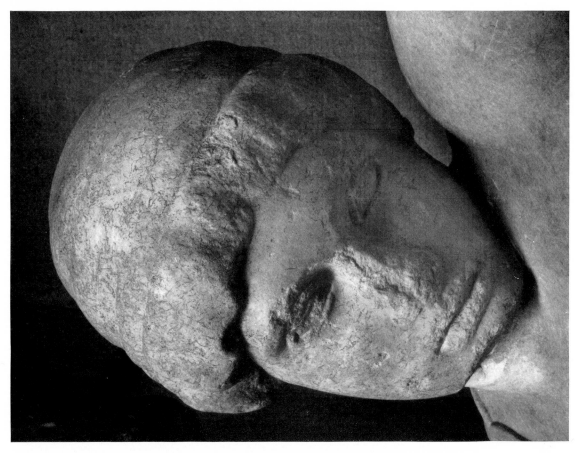

West pediment R

129. Lapith girl

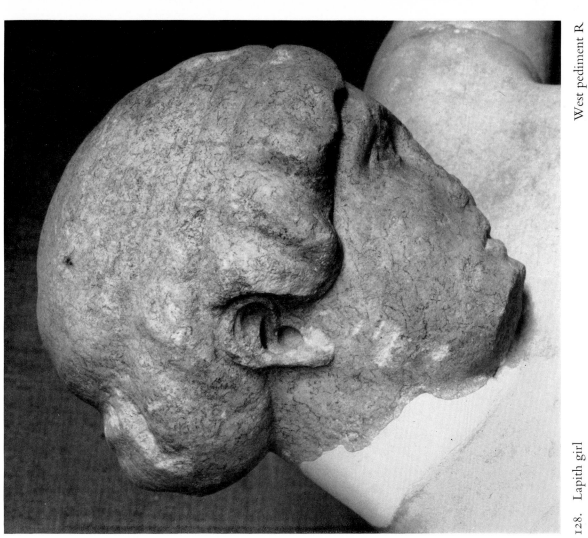

128. Lapith girl

West pediment R

130. Lapith girl

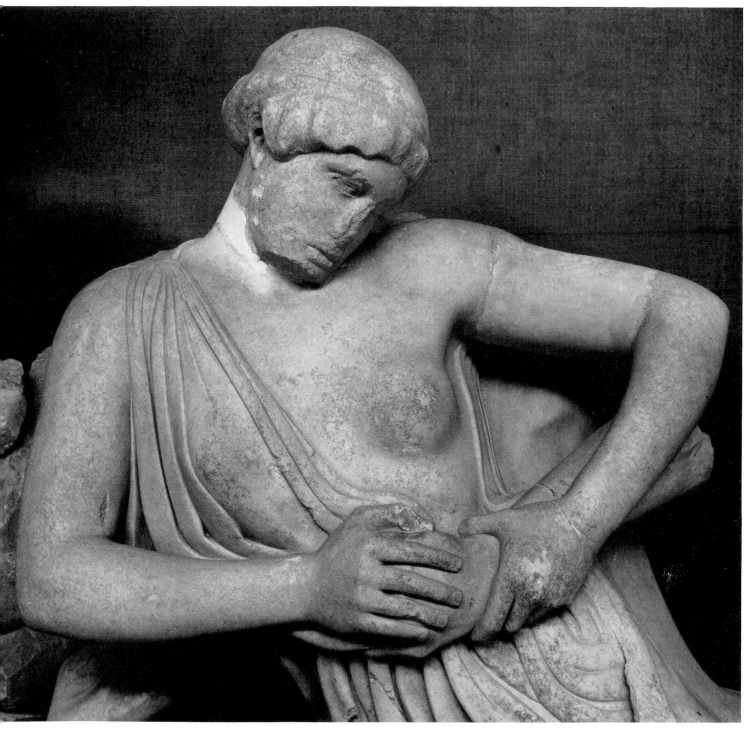

31. Lapith girl

West pediment R

132. Lapith girl

133. Lapith girl

134.   Lapith girl and centaur   West pediment R, S

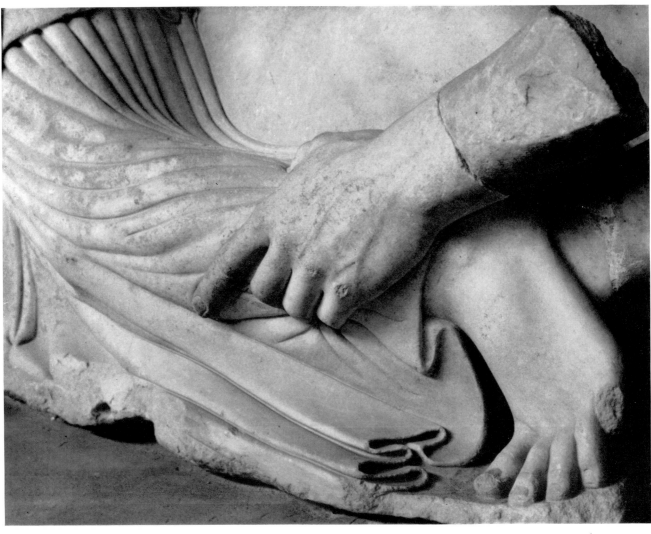

135.   Lapith girl and centaur   West pediment R, S

136. Centaur

137. Centaur

138. Centaur

139.   Centaur and Lapith youth

West pediment S, T

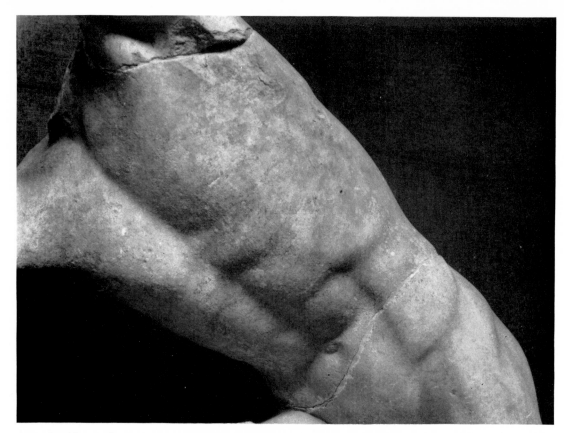

140. Lapith youth   West pediment T

141. Lapith youth   West pediment T

142. Lapith youth

143. The first Labour of Herakles: The lion of Nemea   Metope, West side
      [The lion, except the hindquarters, is in the Musée du Louvre, Paris]

144.　Head of Athena. Detail from plate 143

145-6.   Head of Athena. Details from plate 143

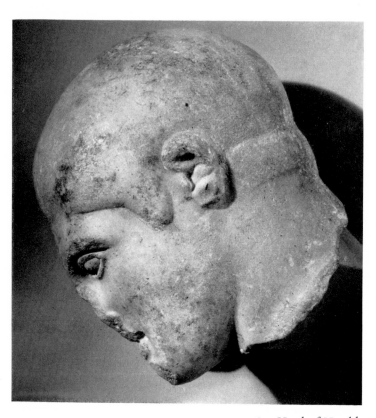

147-8.   Head of Herakles. Details from plate 143

149. Head of Athena. Detail from plate 143

150. Head of the lion [Musée du Louvre, Paris]. See plate 143

151. The lion [Musée du Louvre, Paris]. See plate 143

152. The second Labour of Herakles: The hydra of Lerna

Metope, West side

153. The third Labour of Herakles: The birds of Stymphalos   Metope, West side
   [The figure of Athena, the head of Herakles and his right arm are in the Musée du Louvre, Paris]

154.   Head of Athena [Musée du Louvre, Paris]. See plate 153

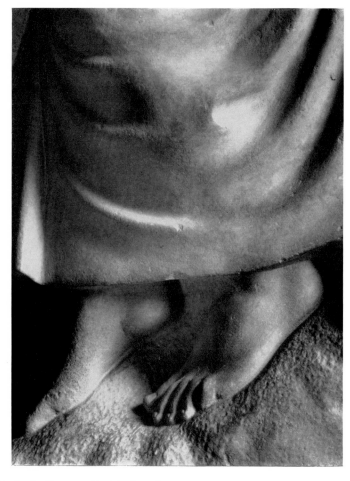

155–6.   Drapery and feet of Athena [Musée du Louvre, Paris]. See plate 153

157.   Athena [Musée du Louvre, Paris]. See plate 153

158–9. Head of Athena [Musée du Louvre, Paris]. See plate 153

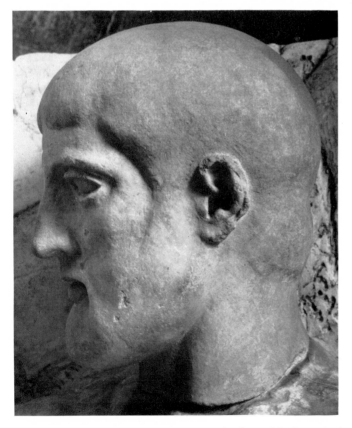

160–1. Head of Herakles [Musée du Louvre, Paris]. See plate 153.

162. The fourth Labour of Herakles: The Cretan bull　　　　　　　　　　　　Metope, West side
　　　[The upper two thirds, except the head of the bull, are in the Musée du Louvre, Paris]

163–4.   Head of Herakles [Musée du Louvre, Paris]. Detail from plate 162

165–6.   Head of the bull. See plate 162

167.   Herakles [Musée du Louvre, Paris]. See plate 162

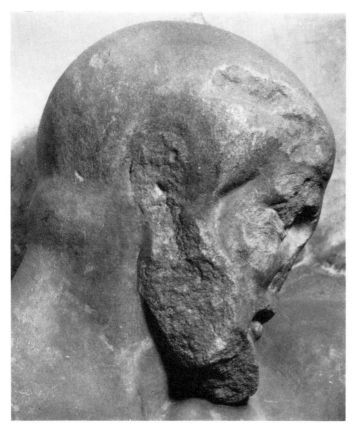

168. Head of Herakles [Musée du Louvre, Paris]
See plate 162

169. Head of Herakles [Musée du Louvre, Paris]
See plate 173

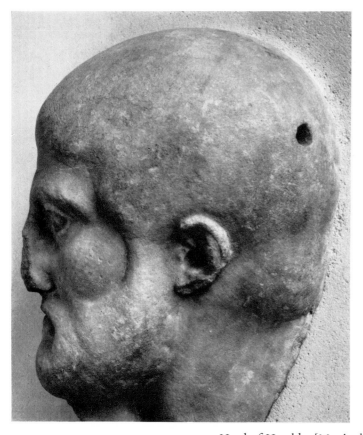

170–1. Head of Herakles [Musée du Louvre, Paris]. See plate 173

172. The fifth Labour of Herakles: The Keryneian hind   Metope, West side
[The head of Herakles and the large fragment on the right have now been transferred to the Amazon Metope, see plate 173]
[The left hand of Herakles is in the Musée du Louvre, Paris]

173.   The sixth Labour of Herakles: The girdle of the Amazon
[The head of Herakles is in the Musée du Louvre, Paris]

Metope, West side

174. The seventh Labour of Herakles: The Erymanthian boar   Metope, East side
[The near half of the head of Eurystheus, the fragment of head, shoulder and right upper arm of Herakles, and the muzzle of the boar are in the Musée du Louvre, Paris]

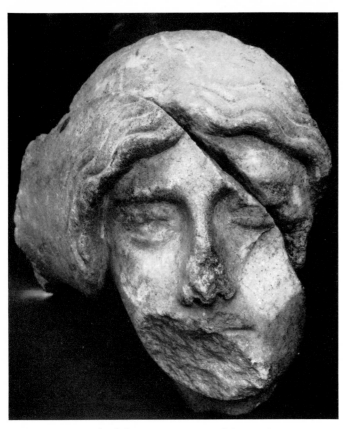

175. Head of the Amazon. Detail from plate 173

176. Head of Eurystheus [Musée du Louvre, Paris]. See plate 174

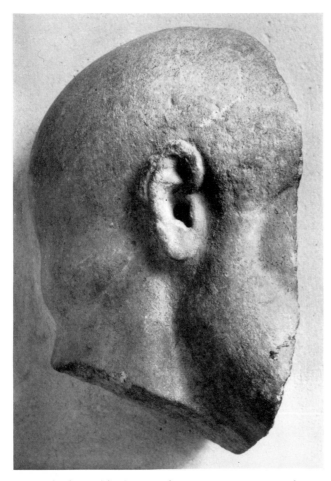

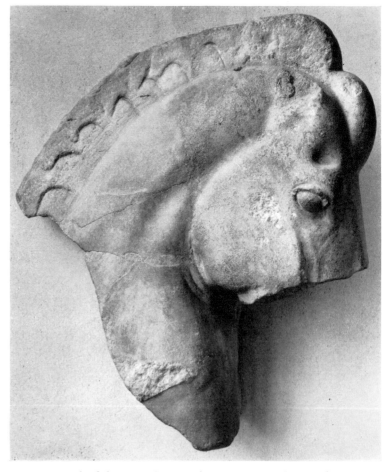

177. Head of Herakles [Musée du Louvre, Paris]. See plate 179

178. Head of the mare [Musée du Louvre, Paris]. See plate 179

179. The eighth Labour of Herakles: The mares of Diomedes   Metope, East side
[The right upper arm and the back of the head of Herakles, and the head of the mare are in the Musée du Louvre, Paris]

180. The ninth labour of Herakles: The fight with Geryon   Metope, East side
      [The near shield of Geryon and his head are in the Musée du Louvre, Paris]

181. Geryon [Musée du Louvre, Paris]. See plate 180

182–3.   Head of Herakles. Details from plate 180

184.   Head of Herakles. Detail from plate 180

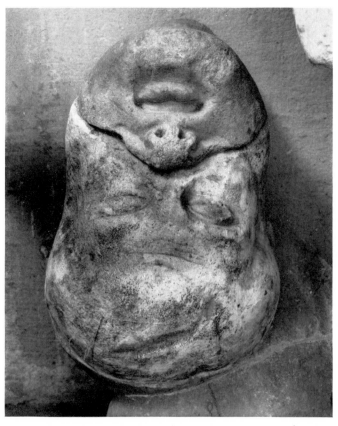

185.   Head of Geryon [Musée du Louvre, Paris]. See plate 180

186.   Herakles. Detail from plate 188

187. Drapery of Athena. Detail from plate 188

188.   The tenth Labour of Herakles: The apples of the Hesperides   Metope, East side

189–90.   Head of Herakles. Details from plate 188

191.   Head of Athena. Detail from plate 188

192.   Head of Atlas. Detail from plate 188

193.   Atlas. Detail from plate 188

194–5. Head of Herakles. Details from plate 198

196–7. Head of Herakles. Details from plate 198

198.   The eleventh Labour of Herakles: The capture of Kerberos   Metope, East side

199. Herakles. Detail from plate 198

200. Torso of Herakles. Detail from plate 198

201. Head of Kerberos. Detail from plate 198

202. The twelfth Labour of Herakles: The stables of Augeias   Metope, East side

203. Athena and Herakles. Detail from plate 202

204. Athena. Detail from plate 202

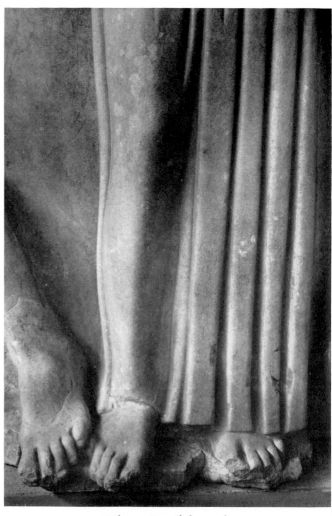

205. Athena. Detail from plate 202

206. Athena. Detail from plate 202

207–8. Head of Herakles. Details from plate 202

209. Herakles. Detail from plate 202

210.   Athena. Detail from plate 202

211. Athena. Detail from plate 202

THE RECOVERY AND RESTORATION OF THE
SCULPTURES: AN HISTORICAL SURVEY
BY NICHOLAS YALOURIS

THE RECOVERY AND RESTORATION OF THE SCULPTURES: AN HISTORICAL SURVEY BY NICHOLAS YALOURIS

BY the year 456 B.C. the two gigantic pedimental compositions had been set within their triangular frames, and the two series of metopes crowned the entrance to the pronaos and the opisthodomos of the temple. For the next ten centuries, these gods and heroes, immortal in stone, were a revelation which stirred the hearts of generation after generation. Pausanias saw them still dominating the precinct when he visited Olympia in the later second century A.D., and it was not until the sixth century A.D. that a violent earthquake destroyed the temple, broke the sculptures into thousands of pieces, and scattered them over the precinct. Ruins and sculptures alike were gradually covered with successive layers of soil, largely alluvial, until the deposit was eventually twenty to thirty feet deep; and protected in this way they lay in safety until the nineteenth century. Then, at Olympia and elsewhere, there began a series of excavations inspired by an awakening interest in the origins of European civilization, and particularly in the remains of Greek antiquity. First came the scholars of the French *Expédition Scientifique de Morée*, who excavated for six weeks in 1829; they reached the stylobate of the temple and found large pieces of three of the metopes and smaller fragments, all of which are now preserved in the Louvre. Some decades later, in 1875, a contract was signed between the governments of Greece and Germany by the terms of which the Germans undertook a systematic investigation of the whole sanctuary. Many hundred thousand cubic feet of soil were gradually removed, to reveal the precinct as it had been after the earthquake of the sixth century: the resulting picture was one of hundreds of architectural members scattered over the whole area, and among them innumerable fragments of sculpture from every ancient period.

Since that time investigators have been faced with a puzzle of appalling complexity. First of all the fragments had to be classified according to whether they came from single statues or from larger compositions, the criteria being the kind of marble, the size of the figures to which they belonged, and the style and quality of the work. Works of earlier and of later periods, down to the Roman, had to be eliminated before it was possible to segregate those pieces which seemed to belong to the sculptures of the temple of Zeus. Then came the endless attempts to fit them together, an exhausting process of trial and error rendered more difficult by the weight of the fragments and by their being in three dimensions, though enlivened from time to time by successes. Seeing the pediments in their present state, one has little idea of the long and laborious efforts necessary to reassemble them, of the despair induced by the bewildering multitude of fragments, or of the enthusiasm that prompted renewed attacks upon the problem. One man, Georg Treu, dedicated a great part of his life to Olympia, and bore the brunt of this task. He could not have carried it to completion, for apart from the fact that many fragments still lay unidentified in the store-rooms of the museum others had never been found at all. In recent years new attempts have been made which have been rendered easier by Treu's work; and indeed any subsequent successes must necessarily be secondary to his great achievement. Just before the war of 1940, E. Kunze and U. Jantzen added a number of pieces, partly from new excavations which had begun in 1936, and partly from unidentified fragments in the store-rooms: the results of this work are published in vol. IV of the *Olympia Bericht*. During the last decade the Greek Archaeological Service has carried on the task, and has added just under two hundred new pieces, of which sixty-eight have been attached to figures in the pediments, and sixty-six to the metopes: sixty-five more have been ascribed with certainty to their original places, but have not been attached because the intermediate parts are missing, and they are not shown either in the plates or in the drawings of this book. Some of these fragments had already been identified by Treu, but had afterwards been overlooked, and so were not attached to the figures during their reconstruction. (See *Bulletin de Correspondance Hellénique*, vol. 80, pp. 28-69; vol. 81, pp. 569-72.)

Valuable though any addition, however small, to an ancient work of art must be, most of the new joins did not alter the composition of the original figures or their arrangement: some few, however, did help towards a better understanding of their style or interpretation; or affected their pose and their position in the pediments or metopes.

THE NEW ADDITIONS: SOME FRESH OBSERVATIONS AND THE CONCLUSIONS TO BE DRAWN FROM THEM

THE EAST PEDIMENT

14 H: Three fragments have been added: the first, under the left hand, consists of part of a piece (made separately and inserted) with vertical folds: the second, with oblique folds of the himation, belongs to the right hip: the third, of large size, and roughly worked, forms part of the drapery of the left side and back, at the level of the knee. The first two fragments were identified by Treu, but have now been attached for the first time.

19 K: The right forearm (not illustrated) attributed to this figure cannot have been outstretched, and therefore cannot have held a phiale as has sometimes been suggested, because the socket in the elbow is not sufficiently large for a dowel to support the arm in this position. If this arm does belong to K, it must have been bent upwards towards her chest.

50-52 B: A small fragment has been added to the back of his head: the surface on its right half, which was outwards, is carefully finished, whilst on its left half traces of tooling with the point remain: these traces extend to the adjacent surface of the left side of the head. The left side of this figure and the left buttock also have a rough finish. Part of the left buttock was trimmed away after the statue had been carved, undoubtedly in order to fit it into the pediment: therefore his left side should face the wall of the pediment. His right arm was not outstretched, but bent in front of the chest, and it reached as high as the left ear, which, being covered and out of sight, is roughly worked. The movement of this arm, and the hole through the fingers for the reins, justify the attribution of this hand to B, and not to P as has also been suggested.

53 D, Chariot-team: Three pieces have been added. Two of them, joining one another, belong to the lower part of the neck and part of the chest of the outer horse, whilst the third, larger piece, belongs to the hip of the second horse from the outside: this fragment was identified by Treu but has now been attached for the first time. Two other pieces, comprising part of the upper jaw of a horse, the nasal bone and the nostrils,

have been fitted to one another: these two pieces, to-gether with another piece from a lower jaw, certainly belong to the outer horse, but they have not been attached because the intermediate portion is missing.

56-57 C: He kneels behind chariot D in profile, as is shown by the unfiinished surface of his left side (towards the wall of the pediment), but with a slight turn of his body outwards, as is shown by the unfinished surface of his back. The turn outwards is confirmed by the fact that the left knee and lower leg are perfectly finished towards the front of their left side.

58 L: Two fragments, adjoining one another, have been added to the left part of the chest. These make it certain that the left shoulder was higher than the right, and that the raised left arm, which leaned on a staff, as in N, supported the weight of the whole torso. The head, now wrongly set, must be lowered three or four centimetres and turned to its left, that is towards the middle of the pediment, so that the cutting on the top of it and the raking ceiling of the pediment are parallel (see p. 174). The turn of the head towards his left must be followed also by a turn of the body rather greater than at present, and just so far as the well-finished and therefore visible surface of the right side of the figure allows: the figure itself, however, still remains frontal.

G: Three pieces identified, but not attached. Two of them, joining one another, complete a large part of the left thigh and left buttock; the third belongs to the right knee. 49

F: Two pieces added. The first, a small one, forms part of the vertical folds just under the right forearm; the second belongs to the plinth under the left foot. 48

M (chariot-team): The right ear of the second horse from the outside has been attached. It is not possible that the portion of a plinth (consisting of three pieces joined, with three hooves upon it, the whole made in one piece) belongs to the hindlegs of the horses, as was believed. It must belong to the forelegs, two of the hooves being those of the second horse from the out-side, and the third being that of the left foreleg of the third horse from the outside. This new arrangement is confirmed by the traces of a support on the plinth behind the middle hoof, corresponding with those on the bellies of the three inner horses. 30

N: A small fragment has been added to the upper part of the chest, just below the right shoulder. 32

THE POSITION OF THE FIGURES IN THE EAST PEDIMENT
(See fig. 15 and folding plate at the end of the book.)

Valuable guidance to the placing of the figures in the pediments is given by the find-spots of their fragments. All the figures assigned to the east and west pediments were found in fragments in the area in front of the east and west façades of the temple respectively: one exception, the right arm of Apollo from the west pediment, was found in front of the east façade. Small fragments could easily have been carried to a distance, but the main portions of the statues are unlikely to have been moved far from the place where they originally fell. Even though many of them were found used in later buildings and not lying as they had fallen, the great accumulation of blocks and sculptures of every size in the area round the temple makes it clear that people would naturally use the abundant material lying close to where they wanted to build, and would not have to bring any from a distance. G. Treu, however (*Olympia*, III, p. 99 ff.), believed that the find-spots of the sculptures for the most part do not correspond with the places where they actually fell, and consequently do not indicate their original position in the pedimental compositions: yet it does seem that other evidence cited below tends to confirm that of the find-spots. Other criteria for the placing of the figures are the height of each figure, which must correspond to that of the raking cornice; the turn to right or left; and the unfinished surfaces that were not intended to be seen.

The figures whose exact positions in the east pediment are indisputable, are these: H: Being the tallest figure in the composition, it necessarily marks the vertical axis of the pediment. A, P: These, and these only, fit the two corners: A, facing right, in the left (south) corner, and P, facing left, in the right (north) corner.

D, M: The two chariot-teams, each of which stands nearly in the middle of each half of the pediment; D, facing right in the left (south) half, and M, facing left in the right half.

L: His position in the left half of the pediment to the left of A is established by the oblique cutting on the top of his head, which was parallel to the raking ceiling of the pediment and was made so that the figure could be set in this position (see p. 173).

The positions of these figures, which are established independently in this way, are corroborated by the places where they were found during the excavations, with one exception, the fragments of the central figure H, which were found partly opposite the north half of the pediment, and partly opposite its south end. The fragments of A were found opposite the south end of the pediment: the torso of P was found opposite the north end, whilst his head and lower legs, being less heavy, were found some distance further away, but still opposite the north end. As for the two chariot-teams, most of the fragments of D were found opposite the southern half of the pediment, those of M partly opposite the northern half (with one fragment opposite the southern), partly N.E. of the north end.

The fact that the positions of these figures, established on independent grounds, are corroborated by the places where they were found, encourages one to study the find-spots of the other figures.

The fragments of G were found partly east of the north half of the pediment and partly N.E. of its north corner, and the fragments of F approximately in the same places. The fragments of I and K were found opposite the south end. Of the remaining figures C, B, O, N, and E (which is smaller than the others) the fragments were found as follows: C's opposite the south half of the pediment: B's opposite the north half and part of it N.E. of the north corner: O's partly opposite the north half and partly N.E. of the north corner: N's (torso and head) in front of the last column but one on the north: E's in front of the first inter-columniation from the north.

Thus the position of each figure in the pediment according to the find-spot, and according to certain other evidence which will be mentioned, is as follows: the couple G F must belong to the north half of the pediment, their exact position, determined by their height, being G beside Zeus and F further out between him and the chariot-team. The couple I K must belong to the south half of the pediment, I by Zeus, K by the chariot-team, again because of their height. N must belong to the north half of the pediment behind the right-hand chariot-team, his position being determined by his turn towards the middle (the back unfinished), and by his height in relation to the ceiling of the pediment. E must occupy the position between P and N, his height being appropriate to this.

O: The find-spot of this figure, although indicating a position in the north half of the pediment, does not justify a more precise location. However, since all the figures of the north half of the composition have now been placed, no other space is left there except that in front of the chariot-team M. Further, according to the ancient tradition, constant during the archaic and classical periods, Pelops did not have a charioteer in the race with Oinomaos because, by the conditions of the contest, Hippodameia accompanied her suitor so as to divert his attention: thus the naming of a charioteer of Pelops by Pausanias must be a later addition to the myth. So it is probable that figure O is a servant of Hippodameia and her nearness to her is thus justified.

C must belong to the south half of the pediment, and his precise position must be behind the chariot, as his height indicates.

B: The find-spot gives no exact indication of the position; but since all the figures in the south half of the composition are now placed, the only space remaining for B is in the front of the chariot-horses D. This is corroborated by the following points: the unfinished state of his left side and the hollowing-out of part of the left buttock (see p. 172) which shows that the figure was close beside another one, in this case the fore-legs of the chariot-team D, in front of which he was kneeling; and, second, the notch on the short right side of the plinth on which are the hooves of the outside horse of the team, justify the assumption that this was cut after it was placed in the pediment, in order to accommodate the right sole of B.

In the identification of the figures and in fixing their position in the pediments we are to some extent helped by Pausanias, although his text is sometimes erroneous, especially in naming the figures, perhaps because he was mis-informed by the guides. His description of the east pediment is fairly detailed: besides mentioning the thirteen figures and the two chariots, which correspond to the number of statues found in front of the eastern façade, he names most of them and gives the subject of the myth. Nevertheless, two phrases used by Pausanias have for many years caused differences of opinion about the positions of the figures. Pausanias, beginning his description from the central figure, Zeus, writes: ἐν δεξιᾷ τοῦ Διός and ἐς ἀριστερὰ ἀπὸ τοῦ Διός and these two phrases can be translated as either 'On Zeus's own right (and left)' or 'On the right (and left) of Zeus from the point of view of the spectator'. The assumption that these phrases refer respectively to the right and left side of Zeus himself is confirmed not only by the literal translation of the passage, but also by the evidence already mentioned, namely, the find-spots and the heights of the figures. Thus the bearded hero, I, whom we have placed on the right of Zeus, cannot be anyone but Oinomaos, and the female figure K, whom we have placed beside him, wearing the austerely architectural Doric peplos, must be his wife Sterope: the raising of the overfall with her left hand serves to identify her. This gesture is familiar in scenes of farewell; therefore it is not appropriate to Hippodameia, who, according to an unvarying tradition, accompanied Pelops in the race. The next figure on our left, B, in heroic nudity, is called Myrtilos by Pausanias. Of the three remaining figures, two, C and L, are not named by Pausanias, while the third, A, is called Kladeos: by those who translate the two phrases differently, this figure is called Alpheios.

18

19

50–52

2

In the other half of the pediment, on the left (our right) of Zeus, Pausanias mentions Pelops,
49   who will be the young beardless hero G; and Hippodameia, who will be F, a maiden with a
48   peplos loosely covering the tender body. The figure next to F, who, according to our arrange-
22-27   ment must be O, kneeling in front of the horses, is called by Pausanias a charioteer (Sphairos
or Killas) perhaps because of her long dress, which resembles that worn by charioteers: it was
no doubt the distance which misled him as to her sex. Pausanias did not know the names
4   of the next two figures (N, E); the last figure (P), now generally called Kladeos, he named
Alpheios. There is however an observation not hitherto adduced in identifying the last two
41-43   figures, E and P, and that is E's striking resemblance to the figure of Arkas, founder-hero of
Arcadia, on a coin of that country (see fig. 11): and if E is in fact Arkas, a position next to P
would be most appropriate, since the river Alpheios rises in Arcadia.

The arrangement of the figures in the east pediment suggested above agrees with the
proposed interpretation of the passage in Pausanias. See fig. 15 and p. 31.

THE COMPOSITION

Of the two groups, one belonging to Oinomaos, the other to Pelops, which are separated and
at the same time united by the central figure of Zeus, that of Oinomaos is placed at the right
hand of Zeus, that of Pelops on his left. Thus Zeus is framed on right and left by the two
spears, symmetrically disposed, held by Oinomaos and Pelops in the left and right hands
respectively: these two spears accentuated the invisible presence of Zeus at the contest, and
separated the human sphere from that of the god. Hippodameia, with one arm bent horizontally
and the other obliquely on the chest in harmonious correspondence with the arms of Pelops,
stands beside him in complete concentration and dramatic immobility: she has in mind the
fatal end which the contest will have either for her father or for her suitor. Beside Oinomaos
stands Sterope, bidding her husband farewell with a characteristic gesture. The position of her
left arm, which is bent on the shoulder and, together with the elbow, moved forward, is
harmoniously connected with the position of the arm of Oinomaos, which is drawn back
with the hand on the hip.

58, 31 The two old men L, N, have been rightly identified with the seers Klytios and Iamos, the
mythical ancestors of the two homonymous families from which the two seers of the Sanctuary
were elected. The placing of them apart in the two groups of the composition has a special
importance and justification. They emphasize the silent presence of the figures, and their
isolation, comparable to that in a tragic drama.

33-34, 36 The expression of the seer N is dark and thoughtful, and that of seer L, before the statue was
59-61   mutilated, must have been similar, presaging the fatal destinies of the two heroes – that of
Oinomaos immediate, that of the dynasty of Pelops more distant but inexorable. Thus the
turn of Zeus's head, which has been assumed by some scholars, was dictated – if it really
existed – by the sculptor's aesthetic or other conception of the structure and balance of the

statue, and does not indicate the outcome of the contest, since neither side was favoured. The presence of E has been briefly discussed above.

The identification by Pausanias of the two corner figures A, P as personifications of rivers   2, 4 has been disputed by some scholars, mainly on the ground that no such humanized reclining rivers are known before the Hellenistic Age. But the fact that such figures are not known in sculpture is not sufficient reason for rejecting the identifications. In other forms of art the replacement of zoomorphic beings, both rivers and others, by human personifications, began in the early fifth century B.C. and developed steadily until it was completed in the classical period. A relevant example is the representation of the river Gelas as a man-headed bull, constant on coins of Gela through most of the fifth century: later (about 415 B.C.) the river is completely humanized, and only the horns recall the original zoomorphic conception. Another example is the representation of Io, who had been changed by Hera into a cow: and as a cow she appears throughout the archaic period until the beginning of the fifth century B.C., when she gradually starts to regain her human form. In the classical period, two horns alone serve to remind us of the original transformation. This is shown both by vase-paintings and by the relevant passages in tragedies by Aeschylus (*Suppliants* 568, written about 475–70 B.C., and *Prometheus Bound* 567, 589, 681 (of uncertain date)). Compare also Herodotos II. 41. The frequency, in the Hellenistic period, of personifications of river-gods reclining merely reflects the preference of that period for figures not in action, and does not prove that such figures did not exist in the classical period. Thus the identification of the two corner figures of the east pediment with the two rivers which brought fertility to the land of Elis is justified.

In the pediment as a whole, figures are turned either slightly or more emphatically towards its vertical axis, so that the general composition is centripetal; and the centripetal movement expressed here by the turn of bodies and heads, or even by their general lines, is familiar in the architectural sculpture and the vase-painting of this period. The straight line is dominant; vertical in the central figures, horizontal in the lateral ones; and sometimes angular: but the wavy or curved line is absent. By small deviations from the centripetal movement (e.g. in F, E) rigid symmetry, extremely rare in Greek art, is effectively avoided. The composition thus gains liveliness, and at the same time the individuality of each figure is stressed by its balanced asymmetry. On the other hand, despite the centripetal movement and individual turning to left or right, the figures keep their frontality, being extended to cover the full width of the pediment. The feeling for three dimensions, with which artists have been much concerned since the beginning of the fifth century B.C., is slight, and the deviation from frontality so little (e.g. in D, M, N) that the composition as a whole has the quality of a relief, in which little perspective or sense of space exists. The sculptor deliberately avoids using perspective, of which he has some knowledge, because the deviation from frontality would lessen the immobility and isolation of the figures, which is essential in accentuating the tragedy latent in the myth.

THE WEST PEDIMENT

103

L: A small fragment has been added to the upper part of the right thigh in front.

K: A piece consisting of the left part of the heel and part of the ankle has been added to the left foot. Another piece has been added to the himation where it falls on the right end of the plinth: the addition of this piece necessitates changing the present position of the left foot by moving it to the left and forward, in front of the newly-attached piece.

110–111

H, I: Sixteen new fragments have been added. Three of them, joining one another, complete most of the chest of the centaur I: the middle and largest of these was found during the German excavation of 1954 and identified then. Another large three-cornered piece fills the gap on the centaur's equine back just below his human chest. The remaining twelve pieces have been attached to H. Ten belong to her drapery as follows: two to the outside of the right thigh; one to the back of the left thigh under the centaur's right foreleg which is curled round behind her; two on the inner (right) side of her left knee; three, joining one another, to the lowest end of her long dress; and two large ones to the drapery falling in front of her left knee. The remaining two fragments are the forefinger and the third finger of her right hand. By the addition of these sixteen pieces these two figures have gained more than any others in the pediments. First, the arrangement of Deidameia's drapery and consequently her twisting movement, have been clarified: and, second, the additions to the centaur's chest make it clear that the plane of his chest was set at an angle to the oblique plane of Deidameia's body in front of him, in such a way as to form an obtuse angle. By these means a new feeling of depth is achieved.

Group M, N, O

92–100

M. Six new fragments have been added: a large one to the upper part of the back on his left, another to the inner (right) part of the left leg just below the knee, where it is covered by the himation; and a third, almost quadrilateral, comprising the outer (left) half of the lowest part of the left leg near the ankle and also covered by the himation. The last piece (which had been ascribed by Treu to the lower edge of the cloak of Apollo) belongs to a larger piece, made separately, which comprised the left part of the lower leg together with the falling himation behind it. The three remaining small fragments belong to the uppermost end of the inserted arms where the dowel for the inserted piece was.

The well-finished surface of the right side of the hero's back, much better preserved on the piece recently added, together with the roughly-finished surface of the left ear, show that the left side of the head and the corresponding upper part of the body have to be turned more towards the back wall of the pediment. On the other hand the excellently-worked surface of the inserted piece on the outer (left) half of the left lower leg shows that the lower half of the body must be turned more towards the front. This turn is corroborated, not only by the oblique position of the left thigh of Theseus, but also by the socket on the rear part near the plinth, which served to fix the statue to the back wall of the pediment: if the proposed turn is made, the socket lies, as it should, parallel to the pediment wall.

N: A piece which includes most of the navel has been added to the right part of the belly.

O: Three small pieces have been added. Two belong to the drapery, one under the left arm, the other near the upper part of the left thigh. The third fragment, which belongs to the lower part of her left leg near centaur N's right foreleg, was identified by Treu but has now been attached for the first time.

Group F, G

G's forelegs were not at an acute angle but fully bent under him so that the front part of his body was nearly on the ground whilst his hindquarters were raised more than in the present arrangement. This is shown by the traces of the left foreleg preserved on the under surface of the thigh.

126

Group P, Q

Q: A small fragment has been added near the left side of the groin. The flat oblong area in the hair above the middle of the forehead is usually described as a puntello: but the oblong shape is unusual for this, and the surface may instead have served for painting or fixing a leaf-like ornament of metal on to a band tied round the head (compare the figures of Lapiths on the krater in New York (fig. 20).

82–9

89   P: Three fragments have been added: the first, a large one, to the left shoulder; the second, a small one, to the right part of the belly just under the chest. A third, oblong piece, belongs to the centaur's right side just below the breast: its lower surface fits the lower surface of the gap there, but its upper surface projects six centimetres: this means that the bend of the centaur's body towards his left is insufficient and must be increased in order to accommodate the new piece exactly in the gap.

72   C: A piece of the tarsus of his left foot has been added.

-77 D: Five pieces have been added. Of these, a large one, wrongly ascribed by Treu to the centaur S, has been fitted to the upper left part of the head. On the left side of this fragment there are well-preserved wavy curls, thicker and longer than those in front. Another piece belongs to the left side of the chest and includes part of the armpit. Two other pieces, joining each other, form the upper-part of the right arm and a little of the armpit. The addition of these two fragments makes it clear that the present position of the head is wrong: it has to be moved into a position which is determined by the fifth piece. This fifth piece, a large one, consists of the hoof of the right foreleg together with the plinth, both made from the same piece of marble: it has now been attached to the far side of the centaur's right hand. By this addition the position of the centaur's right hand is corrected: it was not behind the right foreleg, as Treu assumed, but in front of it, and between it and the left (outer) leg. Consequently the centaur's head, together with his left shoulder, have to be raised and moved forward.

81   E: Three pieces have been added. One fits exactly between the centaur D's hindquarters and the back of E, which are carved from the same block of marble. The two others are small, and belong to vertical folds of the drapery, one above the right breast, the other below it.

127 R: Two fragments have been added to her drapery on the plinth.

70   V: Two fragments of drapery have been added, one above the left knee, the other in the middle of the plinth.

-64, A, B, and U: It has generally been accepted that the
-69 three corner figures made of Pentelic marble, instead of Parian like the other sculptures of the temple, were not contemporary with the rest of the pedimental statues, but were carved later to replace originals which had been destroyed either by one of the earthquakes which are frequent at Olympia or in some other way.

Comparison with the lion-head gutter-spouts of the temple gives valuable help in dating these substituted figures. The original lion-heads, of Parian marble, were largely replaced, as time went on, by others made of Pentelic, except in the fourth century B.C. when the new heads were in Parian: it seems that replacements were necessary no less than nine times, after damage by successive earthquakes or other causes. The fact that the later lion-heads (figs. 9-10) are not accurate copies of the originals but are influenced by the style of their own times, allows them to be compared with A, B, and U, which also reflect the stylistic developments of the periods to which they belong.

B and U are similar to one another in structure and sculptural quality and are therefore contemporary, whilst both differ substantially from A. A shows all the characteristics of works of the fourth century B.C. – the toolmarks left on the surface of body and drapery, the way in which the locks above the right ear are rendered with shallow rough grooves, and finally the eyes, which though similar in form to the eyes of the original statues in the pediment, have a melting quality characteristic of fourth-century work. A group of lion-heads of similar workmanship is now unanimously dated to the fourth century B.C. (fig. 9); they must, like A, have been made after a severe earthquake or other catastrophe in the first half of the century which also caused the collapse of parts of the raking cornice and other architectural members of the temple, fragments of which were found during excavations under the foundation of the Leonidaion, the hostel of the Sanctuary, and elsewhere. This building dates from the second half of the fourth century B.C., and it thus becomes clear that the statues had been damaged before 350 B.C. Furthermore, it seems that at the same time the right arm of V, the figure in the extreme south corner of the pediment, was shattered, probably by the collapse of the raking cornice, and replaced by the inserted arm carved from Pentelic marble, which is still preserved.

The two figures B, U, apparently contemporary with one another but by different hands, were made at a later time than A, as is shown by the realistic features, withered skin, stylized dress, and pathetic expression. Work of the same character with the same kind of tool-marks, and, last but not least, in Pentelic marble of the same quality, with glittering veins of schist, can be seen in another group of lion-heads, and since these date from the first century B.C. (fig. 10), the same date may be proposed for B and U, as some scholars have already suggested by comparing them with other works of the first century B.C.

64, 66
67, 68

62, 63

65

64, 66

THE POSITION OF THE FIGURES IN THE WEST PEDIMENT
(See figs. 16 and 17.)

Although the description by Pausanias is brief, and sometimes erroneous in the naming of the main figures (see p. 31), the arrangement of them is less problematic here than in the east pediment. The position of almost all the figures is determined by their height, by the unfinished surface of the backs, and especially by the fact that many of them are in groups of two or three carved from the same block of marble. This fact, however, caused them to break into more numerous pieces, which were scattered more widely than those from the east pediment; hence the find-spots do not offer so precise a criterion for their original positions. Nevertheless, disagreement is limited to the placing of the groups H, I, K; M, N, O; F, G, and P, Q. The position proposed for F, G, and P, Q (see p. 178) is substantiated by the fact that the right hind foot of centaur S fits exactly into the hollow on the short right side of the plinth of Lapith Q: this hollow was apparently made for this purpose, for the Lapith Q is thus brought nearer to the adjacent Lapith woman R, and the otherwise unavoidable gap between them is filled. Further, the body of centaur G, who kneels with his forelegs on the ground and raises his hindquarters and hindlegs (see p. 178), was never complete behind: in the new arrangement the absence of this part would be concealed by the buttocks of Deidameia. In the arrangement proposed for the groups H, I, K; M, N, O, the height of the figures corresponds better to the raking cornices of the pediment. Further, Apollo's right arm would now be stretched out above the shoulder of Peirithoos (K), demonstrating the active support which is being given him by the god of reason and light. That this figure is Apollo is shown by the traces of the bow which he held, by his godlike posture, by his position in the pediment, analogous to that of Zeus in the east pediment, and by his presence in another centauromachy, that on the frieze of the temple at Bassae, where, with his sister Artemis, he comes to the assistance of the Lapiths.

The identification of K and M, who flank Apollo, with Peirithoos and Theseus, is established by contemporary vase-paintings of the subject, where the two heroes are represented in postures similar to these (see figs. 20, 21). Moreover, on the mixing-bowl in Vienna (fig. 22) the inscription Peirithoos above a figure with a sword and in a pose similar to K, establishes K as the king of the Lapiths.

THE COMPOSITION

Here also, as in the east pediment, the composition is centripetal, but far differently contrived – figures no longer immovable and paratactically disposed, but locked in groups of twos and threes and forming a unity, but one dramatically turbulent. There is nothing here of the tragic immobility of heroes who foresee with foreboding the onset of evil, or sense its approach: here there is dramatic conflict at its climax. Here there are no vertical or horizontal lines:

Fig. 19. Amphiaraos leaving to join the expedition against Thebes. Corinthian krater, about 550 B.C. Formerly Berlin Museum, now destroyed. (a) after Furtwängler-Reichhold, *Griechische Vasenmalerei*, pl. 121–2; (b) from the vase.

Fig. 20. Fight between Lapiths and Centaurs at the wedding feast of Peirithoos. Athenian krater by the 'Painter of the Woolly Satyrs', about 450 B.C. New York, Metropolitan Museum.

Fig. 21. Theseus in the fight between Lapiths and Centaurs. Athenian krater by the 'Niobid Painter', about 460 B.C. Berlin, Staatliche Museen, Antiken-Abteilung.

Fig. 22. Peirithoos in the fight between Lapiths and Centaurs. Athenian krater by the 'Nekyia Painter', about 440 B.C. Vienna, Kunsthistorisches Museum.

Fig. 23. Herakles brings the Erymanthian boar to Eurystheus. Athenian wine-cup by Onesimos, about 480 B.C. London, British Museum.

Fig. 24–5. Herakles supports the heavens; Atlas brings the apples of the Hesperides. Athenian lekythos by the 'Athena Painter', about 480 B.C. Athens, National Museum.

the gigantic bodies, in cross-shaped compositions, tower against each other, counterbalanced in a reckless and desperate struggle.

The centripetal composition, more lively here, is pervaded by a rhythmical, wavy transition from body to body, which rises towards the centre, where it reaches its peak, and falls again gradually until it fades out at the corners. The frontality of the individual figures and of the whole composition is no longer consistent: everywhere there is evidence of the sculptor's repeated attempts to break it and thus to enhance his presentation of an essentially turbulent scene. Almost all the figures, and especially the two groups H, I, K and M, N, O, are set more or less obliquely to the pediment wall and are moreover themselves composed in two planes. Deidameia (H) with the counterpoint of her composition, and with her movement, shows a 110-117 new approach to the conquest of the third dimension: here the sculptor shows himself a pioneer, half a century at least ahead of his time. He had no direct followers, and this twisting movement was not definitely adopted in Greek art until the end of the fifth century, when it led to the break-up of frontality and the realization of the third dimension, with all its consequences. Yet this sculptor's attack on the problem is tentative, since his figures, despite their torsions and their oblique settings, remain essentially frontal.

This is the first time that a centauromachy appears in a pedimental composition: and, further, this is the first time that this version of the centauromachy, where the fight breaks out in the home of Peirithoos as he celebrates his wedding with Deidameia, begins to appear in art. This myth, which symbolizes the struggle of man against the force of untamed nature, expresses admirably the purpose of the contests which were organized in the Sanctuary; and its representation in a dominant place on the temple was, in a sense, a proclamation of the ideals of the Olympic Games.

THE METOPES

THE HYDRA OF LERNA

152 Two large pieces, which fit together, have been added: the surface is battered. They belong to the lower half of the slab, above the lower part of the body of the monster, which goes upwards from left to right. The addition of these two pieces not only connects two large sections of the metope, each consisting of numerous fragments, but also fixes the exact position of the many-headed hydra within the square of the metope.

THE BIRDS OF STYMPHALOS

153 Two fragments have been added. One, fairly large, completes the lower part of the right thigh of Herakles and rectifies the position of the lower leg. The other is a small part of the calf of the left leg.

THE CRETAN BULL

Two small fragments have been added, one to the belly 162 of the bull near the left hip of Herakles, the other to its genitals.

THE KERYNEIAN HIND

Two new pieces have been joined to this metope: a 172 large one, to the lower right corner of the slab; the other, consisting of part of the plinth with the tarsus and toes of a left foot, probably belongs to the Herakles of this metope: it was identified by Treu. Traces of the elbow of a right arm, in the angle formed by the neck and body of the hind, which have so far escaped notice, prove to be decisive in fixing the position of the right arm of Herakles.

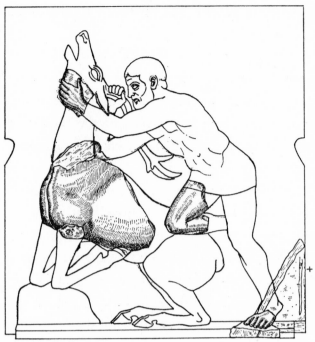

THE KERYNEIAN HIND. Compare plate 172

Two pieces previously assigned to this metope cannot belong to it. One is the head of Herakles, which cannot belong here because there are clear traces of another right arm on the right side of the face: the second is the greater part of a left leg, which cannot belong because the side less well-finished, and therefore intended to be out of sight, would be in view. Both these pieces belong to the metope of the Amazon.

THE GIRDLE OF THE AMAZON

173   The composition of this metope has been greatly changed by recent additions and discoveries. In all, nine pieces have been attached or ascribed to it. Three new pieces have been added to the fragment, closest to the thigh of Herakles, on which is preserved part of the inside edge of a shield: the largest fits to the left of it. On this largest fragment there is part of the inside of an oval shield, the standard type for an Amazon, as well as traces of three fingers on its left side. The position of these four fragments on the upper left side of the metope is established by the preservation on two of them of part of its left edge, with the notch below which served for lifting the metope into position on the building. Below these four fragments has been set another large one, on which are traces of the lower part of the inside of the same shield, with traces of a left arm. Its position is established by two facts: first, the outline of the shield on the other four fragments is continued on

this one; second, this one is of the same thickness, has similar tooling on its back, and preserves part of the original edge of the metope which lines up with the edge of the fragments above it. There can be no doubt that this shield and the left arm and fingers belong to the Amazon: their position and the Amazon's head, with its half-closed eyes and hair falling vertically, show that she had been mortally wounded and had fallen to the ground, still holding the shield above her. The curved outline on the left edge of the fragment correctly identified by Treu as belonging to the right upper part of this metope, was thought to be the outline of a shield held by Herakles. But Herakles usually carries club or bow, or both, rarely a shield; and a new fragment identified as part of an arm has now been fitted on what was thought to be the outline of the shield: this must be the left arm of Herakles. On the same piece of the slab the rough area, oblong in shape, was rightly thought to be the unfinished surface covered by the end of the club of Herakles.

As stated above, the head of Herakles formerly ascribed to the metope of the hind, must belong to this metope. The traces of a missing right arm on the right side of the face show that this arm was bent behind the head and raised threateningly with the club. The position of the arm, and the consequent position of the club, correspond to the oblong rough area on the fragment just described. Two other large fragments, which fit together, preserve part of the buttocks of Herakles in relief: these

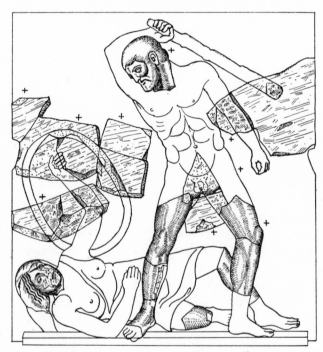

THE GIRDLE OF THE AMAZON. Compare plate 173

are ascribed to this metope because the thickness of the slab and the tooling on the back of it are similar to the other fragments of the metope. Finally, the left leg ascribed by Treu to the metope of the hind must belong here: it is similar in quality of work, and measurements, to the right leg correctly assigned to this metope.

THE ERYMANTHIAN BOAR

174 Five pieces have been added. The first, a large one, with part of a tree-trunk in relief, belongs to the lower left part of the slab: the quality of the work, the thickness of the slab and the tooling on the back of it confirm the attribution. It is further substantiated by comparison with a nearly contemporary painting on a cup by Onesimos in the British Museum (fig. 23). The great similarity, both of the compositions and of the figures of the two protagonists in the painting and the sculpture, made it likely that at least one tree would appear on the metope.

Another large fragment of the slab has been attached above the fragment which has the left thigh of Herakles in relief: on the upper part of this new fragment there are traces of the chiton of Herakles. A third fragment, covered with folds of drapery, belongs to the buttocks of Herakles: this fragment is shown below in a drawing; and the right thigh of Herakles, first identified by Treu and lately rediscovered in the store-rooms of the museum, is also shown only in the drawing. Another small fragment belonging to the lower part of the right leg of Herakles was also identified by Treu, but has now been attached for the first time.

THE MARES OF DIOMEDES. Compare plate 179

THE MARES OF DIOMEDES

Thirteen pieces have been added. The first two belong   179
to the right forearm of Herakles, and though identified by Treu, have now been attached for the first time. Three other fragments, all joining, belong to the upper part of his right shin. Another large fragment, together with a smaller one joining it, forms part of the right hip of Herakles and of the thigh. His left hand, holding the bridle close to the mare's mouth, was identified by Treu but has now been attached for the first time. To the mare has been added a piece comprising the lower jaw, the lips, the tongue, and part of the upper jaw: these are ascribed to this metope because of the quality of the work, the scale, and the kind of marble; and because this is the only metope with a horse: moreover, the hole for the mare's reins in the appropriate fragment corresponds exactly to the hole in the left hand of Herakles. Two other fragments belong to the chest of the mare; and another large piece of the lower left corner of a metope is assigned here because traces on the surface correspond in measurements with a piece of a horse's tail identified by Treu.

THE APPLES OF THE HESPERIDES

Four fragments have been added: one small oblong   188
piece to the front of the lower part of the right thigh of Atlas above the knee. Two other pieces, fitting together, belong to the slab of the metope, the first behind the lower left leg of Atlas, the second behind his right leg, from the thigh to the top of the shank.

THE ERYMANTHIAN BOAR. Compare plate 174

The fourth piece comprises most of the lower part of the left leg. The last three fragments were identified by Treu, but have now been attached for the first time. This labour is depicted in strikingly similar fashion on a rather earlier vase-painting in Athens (figs. 24-25). As with the metope of the boar, so here, it seems that vase-painting and metope were based on the same prototype; and this raises the question of the sources from which the sculptor drew his inspiration.

THE CAPTURE OF KERBEROS

198 Seventeen fragments have been added. One comprises the right side of the neck of Herakles with the upper part of the sternal notch. Four fragments, joining each other, complete much of the right side of Herakles from the arm-pit to the hip: a very small fragment of drapery has been added on the same side, at the top of the thigh, a little lower than the four fragments just mentioned. Six other small fragments, joining one another, complete most of the inside and part of the back of Herakles' right thigh. Another small oblong piece has been added to the left arm-pit of Herakles. To Kerberos three new fragments have been added. Two of them, joining one another, form part of the right side of the head (that towards the background of the metope) and part of the right eye-socket: the third is also on the right side of the head, touching the background. Finally, a fragment has been added which comprises most of the tarsus of the left foot of Hermes, with part of the plinth in one piece with it.

THE STABLES OF AUGEIAS

Ten fragments have been added, five of which belong to the main slab of the metope as follows: The first, triangular in shape, is in the space between the knees of Herakles: the second, also triangular, in the space between the parallel left forearm of Herakles and right arm of Athena. On to this piece the left forearm fits, so that its exact position has now been established. The third piece, again triangular, is on the left side of the slab near the right shoulder of Herakles: at the lowest end of this fragment there remains part of the notch which, together with the corresponding notch on the right side of the metope, was used for lifting and perhaps fastening the slab to the entablature. The fourth piece, on which there are traces of a lower leg, belongs to the lower left side of the slab, behind the lower part of the right leg of Herakles, which fits these traces exactly. The fifth piece belongs above and behind the right shoulder of Herakles. The first three pieces were identified by Treu, but are now attached for the first time: the fourth, found during the German excavations of 1954, was identified by Willemsen.

Of the five remaining pieces, one, which had already been identified by Treu, belongs to the advanced right thigh of Herakles, but the original smooth surface is preserved only on part of the front and on a thin strip at the back of the fragment. Another piece completes the hip of Herakles, whilst the remaining three small pieces, all joining, belong to the inside of his right lower leg.

202

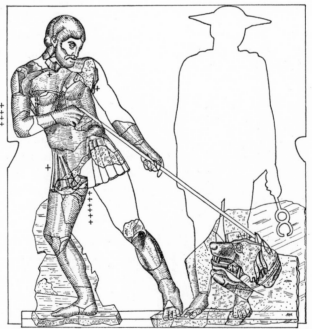

THE CAPTURE OF KERBEROS. Compare plate 198

THE ARTIST

The identity of the artist who designed the sculptures still remains an enigma. They have been assigned at one time or another to almost every sculptor and every school of sculpture of the period, and the problem is complicated by the fact that they seem to combine harmoniously elements deriving from the most varied sources – Attic, Argive, Ionian, South Italian, and others. Yet the general style, the feeling for form, and certain features of the technique, are unique in Greek sculpture, and the individual figures do not resemble any other surviving statues. Further, there seems to be little stylistic connection with works of the periods preceding or succeeding their own, and consequently no indication of either ancestors or descendants. Of late, however, many scholars have come to accept the hypothesis of a Peloponnesian school, and since the architect of the temple, Libon, was an Elean, more specifically of one located in Arcadia or Elis.

But whatever the final solution of this problem, the fact remains that the artist who designed the sculptural decoration and undoubtedly made some of the figures himself, though profoundly conscious of the achievements of other schools, was in his own right an impressive pioneer. His intense and creative temperament enabled him to take cognizance of the artistic tendencies and experiments of his time, whilst his mind was pervaded with the philosophic and poetic ideas of the exuberant generation of the Persian Wars, and thus he could not only assimilate and recreate the ideas of his contemporaries, but in some of his figures he was able to surpass them and to reveal a new horizon: as has been remarked above, the group of Deidameia and Eurytion (H, I, in the west pediment) shows an advance towards the conquest of three-dimensional space which was not repeated immediately and not developed further until about half a century later. Other novel elements have already been remarked by scholars: the lyric or idyllic atmosphere which, to the exclusion of the epic aspects of the deed, pervades the metope of the Stymphalian birds, with the goddess of war unarmed and barefoot: or, in a period distinguished by its love of action, the hero not fighting the lion but exhausted after the fight, a subject which excited no interest otherwise for a hundred years.

The artist was not indebted to sculptors only. The influence of monumental painting is also obvious, and this has led one scholar to maintain that the artist was himself a painter, Panainos. Even if we reject this surmise, we can admit the influence of two great innovators in painting, Kimon of Kleonai, a generation earlier, and especially of Polygnotos, whom ancient writers credited with the first expression of *ethos* in Greek art. This feeling of *ethos*, which succeeded the archaic smile, affects all the figures on the temple both positively and negatively: in the centaurs we are conscious of it by its very absence. The artist's connection with painting is corroborated by numerous vase-pictures, whose similarity to the pedimental compositions and to certain of the metopes (figs. 20-25) proves the debt that both owe to monumental paintings·

The powerful figures of the east pediment, with the stillness of tragedy, hold their pent-up energy in balance: in the west pediment, by contrast, the unleashed energy bursts out like a storm and permeates the whole composition – two different ways of expressing tragedy, equally grand, and equally worthy of this great unknown artist.

Similar contrasts appear in the metopes. In some of them the figures are set vertically and the interest is concentrated: in others the movements are impetuous and the compositions pyramidal or cruciform.

Earlier scholars rightly recognized in these compositions the influence of Attic tragedy, and likened them to Aeschylean plays written in marble. And it is true that these figures no longer narrate the myths as did archaic works: under the influence of tragedy and of the prevailing spirit of the age, myths become simply the medium for the expression of ideas and feelings. As in tragedy, so here, each figure no longer tells the story, but, like an actor, plays his part, whether it be that of chorus or of protagonist.

N.Y.

BIBLIOGRAPHY

The number of books and articles on the sculptures of the temple of Zeus at Olympia is very great. All depend on the original publication by the German excavators, *Die Ausgrabungen zu Olympia*, Berlin, 1875–81, by E. Curtius, F. Adler, and others, in five volumes, of which vol. III, by G. Treu, contains the sculptures of the temple. Treu also discussed the find-spots of the fragments in *Jahrbuch des deutschen archäologischen Instituts*, IV, 1889, p. 266 ff., and the technique and colouring of the sculptures in the same journal, X, 1895, p. 1 ff.

Another major publication of the sculptures of the temple is *Die Skulpturen des Zeustempels zu Olympia*, by E. Buschor and R. Hamann, Marburg, 1924.

Of other works, three general introductions to Olympia may be mentioned: B. Leonardos, *Olympia* (in Greek), Athens, 1901, and *Olympia: its history and remains*, by E. Norman Gardiner, Oxford, 1925, both of them still useful though in some respects out of date; and *Olympia*, by G. Rodenwaldt and W. Hege, Berlin, 1936, more general, but with some fine pictures.

Of these and of the other publications up to 1943, G. Becatti gives an analytical bibliography in *Il maestro di Olimpia*, Firenze, 1943. This excellent book contains not only the relevant quotations from ancient authors, and reproductions of most of the vase-pictures that have a bearing on the sculptures, but also a conspectus of the various reconstructions of the pediments.

Below is given a list of some of the writings since 1943: the most important is no. 5, a thorough and perceptive work based on long study of the sculptures, with emphasis on the evidence of technique as a means of dating the original carvings and the subsequent repairs, and on the evidence of foreshortening and optical adjustments as a guide to the arrangement of the pedimental figures.

1. E. Kunze and U. Jantzen, *Olympia Bericht*, IV, 1940–41 (published 1944), pp. 143 ff.

2. H. Kaehler, 'Das griechische Metopenbild', München, 1949.

3. G. Lippold, *Griechische Plastik:* (Otto-Herbig, *Handbuch der Archäologie* VI. 3. 1.), München, 1950, p. 119 ff.

4. L. Alscher, 'Kompositionsgesetze der Olympiameister: *Mitteilungen des Deutschen Archäologischen Instituts*', vol. 4, 1951, p. 65 ff.

5. S. Stucchi, 'La decorazione figurata del Tempio di Zeus ad Olimpia': *Annuario della Scuola Archeologica di Atene*, vol. 30–32 (N.S. XIV–XVI), 1952–54, p. 75 ff.

6. M. Floriani Squarciapino, 'Pelope e Ippodamia nel frontone orientale di Olimpia': *Annuario (loc. cit.* in no. 5), p. 131 ff.

7. F. Willemsen, 'Die Löwenkopf-Wasserspeier vom Dach des Zeustempels': *Olympische Forschungen*, IV, 1959. (Reviewed by O. Broneer, *American Journal of Archaeology*, vol. 65, 1961, p. 73 f.)

8. B. Ashmole, 'Some nameless sculptors of the 5th century B.C.': *Proceedings of the British Academy*, vol. 48, 1962, p. 214 ff.

9. W. H. Schuchhardt, 'Inhalt und Form bei den Olympia-Metopen': *Festschrift für Hugo Friedrich*, Frankfurt am Main, 1965, p. 239 ff.

10. C. Kardara, Στερόπη καὶ Ἱπποδάμεια: *Ephemeris*, 1965, pp. 168 ff.

On the statue of Zeus and the workshop of Pheidias, the latest writings are:

11. W. H. Schuchhardt, 'Die Niobidenreliefs vom Zeusthron in Olympia': *Mitteilungen des Archäologischen Instituts*, 1 (1948), pp. 95-137.

12. C. Morgan, 'Pheidias and Olympia' in *Hesperia*, vol. 21, 1952, p. 295 ff.

13. J. Liegle, 'Der Zeus des Pheidias', Berlin, 1952.

14. C. J. Herington, *Papers of the British School at Rome*, vol. 26, 1958, p. 41 ff. (on a possible copy of the Zeus, at Cyrene).

15. E. Kunze, *Neue deutsche Ausgrabungen im Mittelmeergebiet und im Vorderen Orient*, Berlin, 1959, p. 263 ff.

16. A. Mallwitz u. W. Schiering, 'Die Werkstatt des Pheidias in Olympia': *Olympische Forschungen*, v, 1964. (Reviewed by A. M. Snodgrass, *Journal of Hellenic Studies*, vol. 85, 1965, p. 238 ff.)

o)
f Oinomaos
s)

N (31–40)
Seer, perhaps Iamos

E (41–43)
Seated boy, perhaps Arkas

P (1, 4–12)
River-god (Kladeos or Alpheios)

THE WEST PEDIMENT

R, S (127–139)
Lapith girl and centaur

T (127, 139–142)
Lapith youth

U (66, 68)
Old Lapith woman

V (65, 70)
Lapith woman

The sculptures of the East and West pediments as displayed in the Museum of Olympia, 1965.—Numbers in brackets refer to the plates.